THANK YOU FOR YOUR ORDER!

If you had a positive experience with our book, we ask you to leave a review,

it would be very important for us!

THANK YOU
THANK YOU
THANK YOU
THANK YOU
THANK YOU

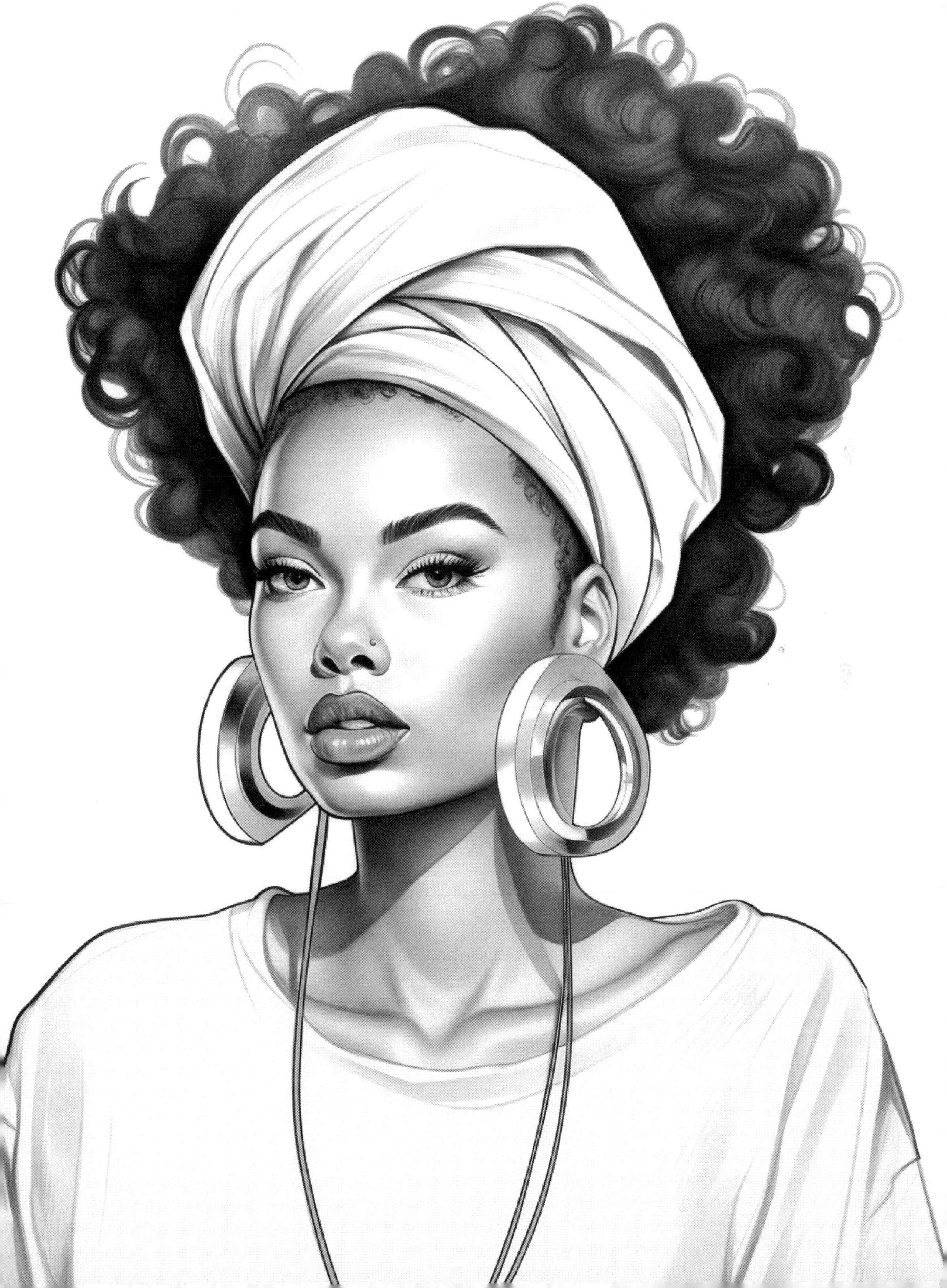

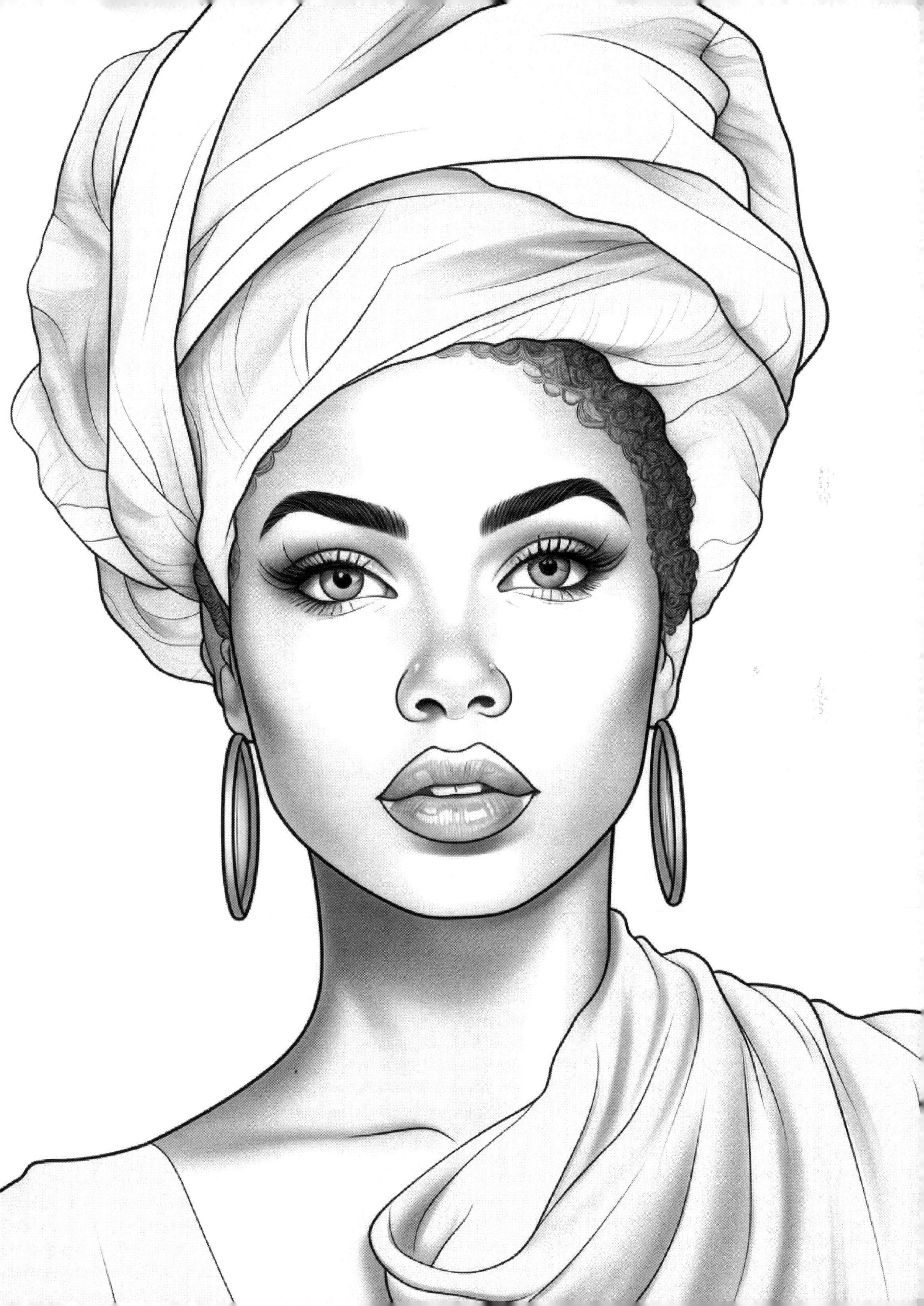

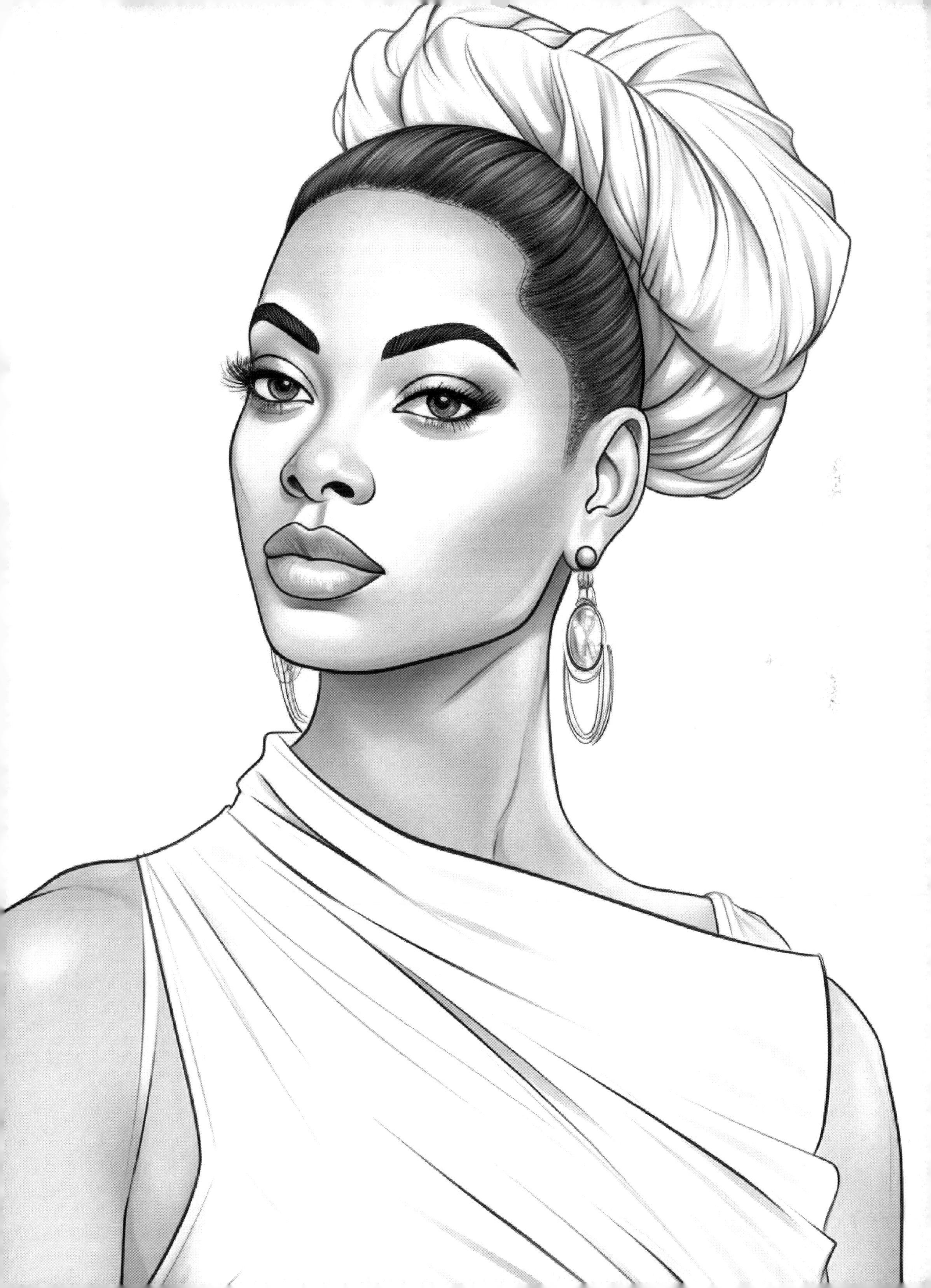

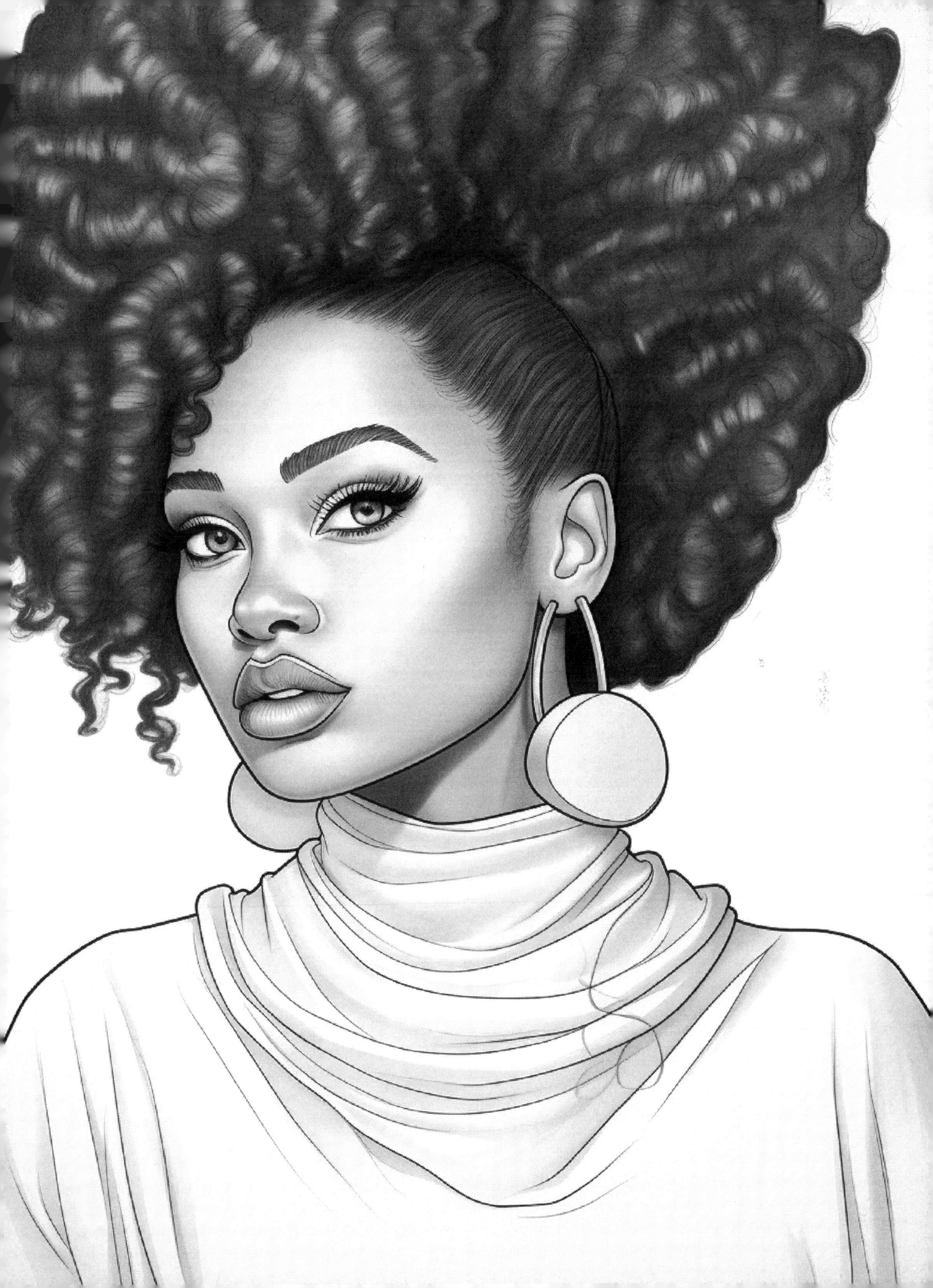

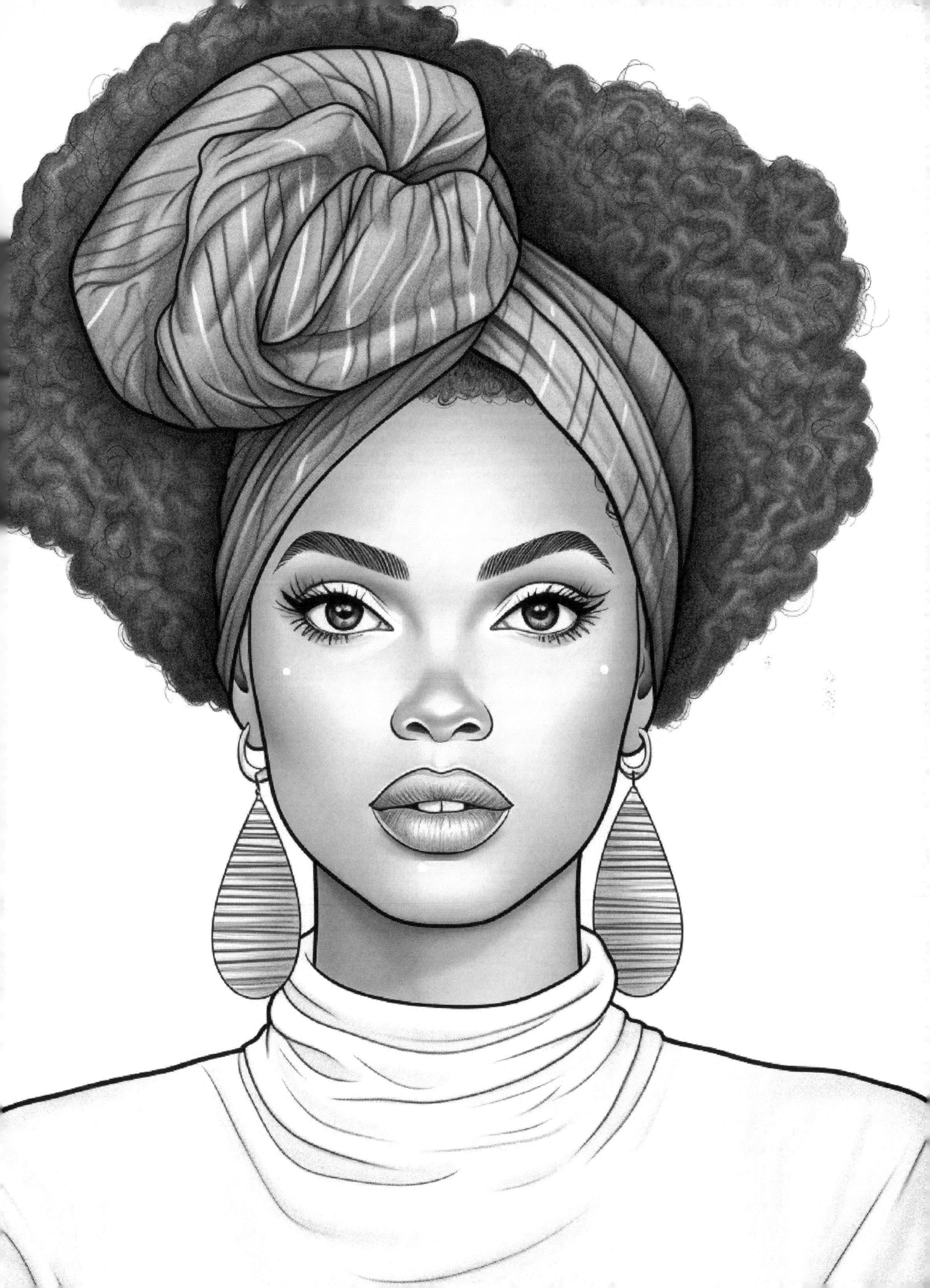

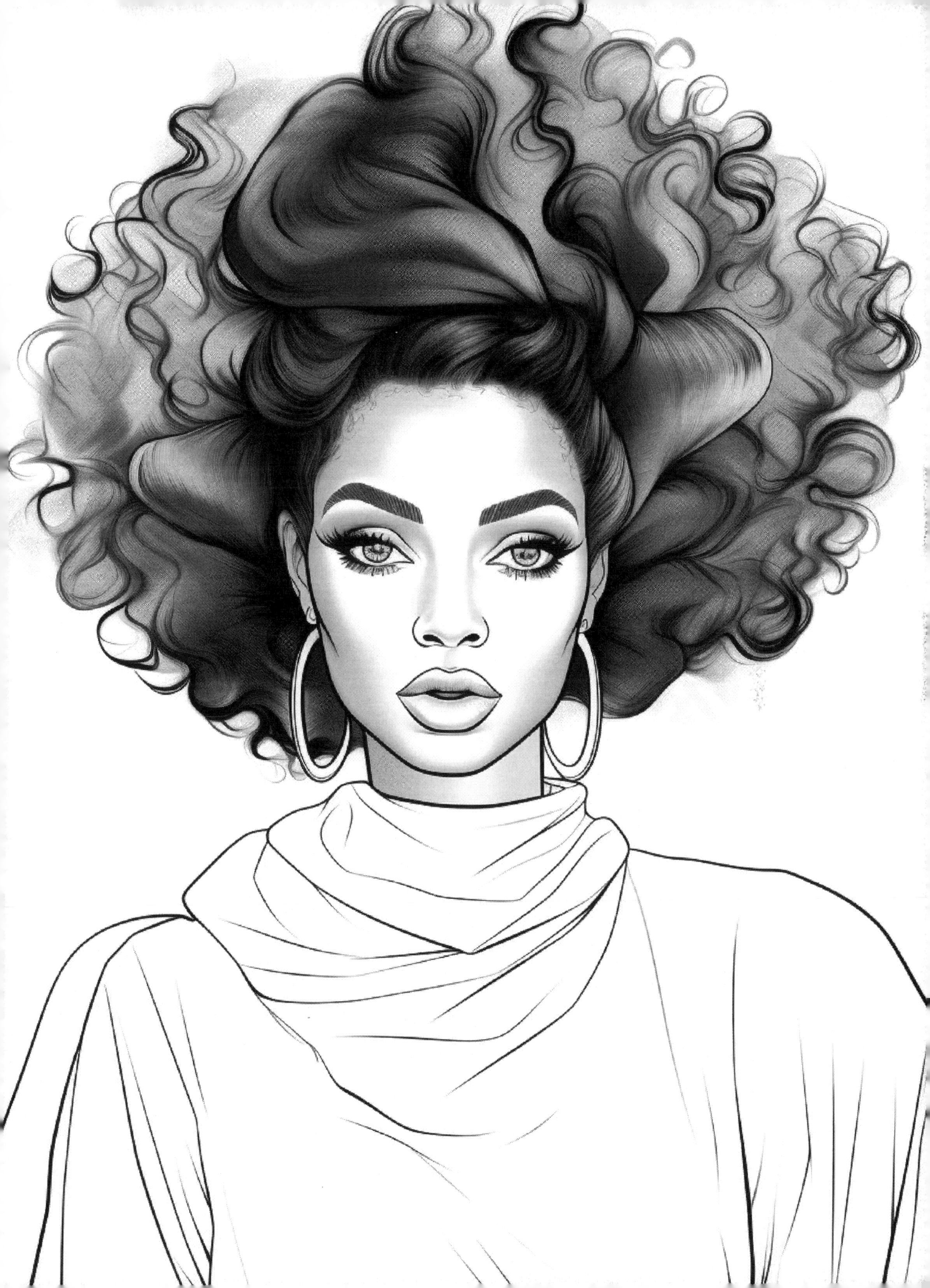

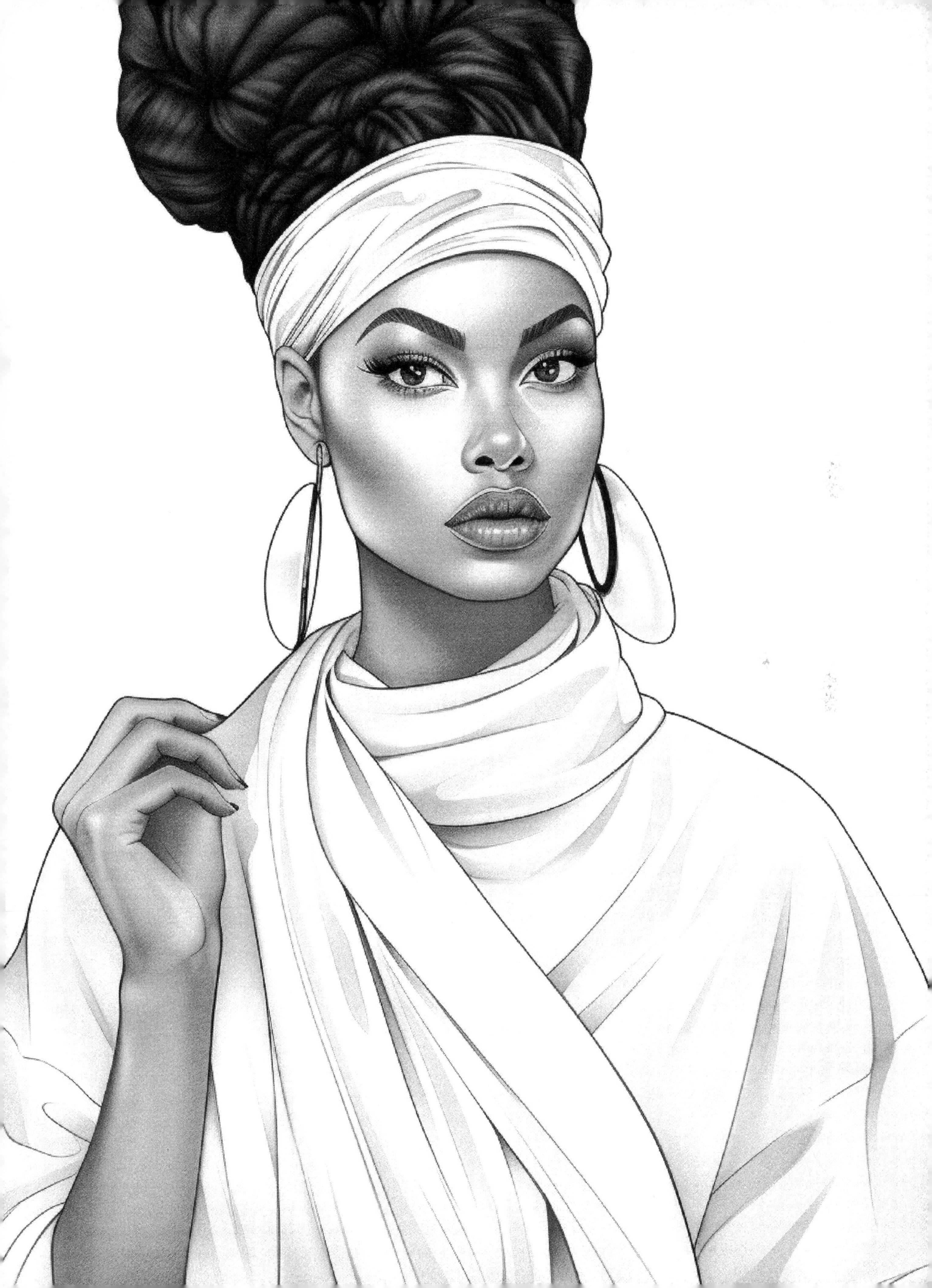

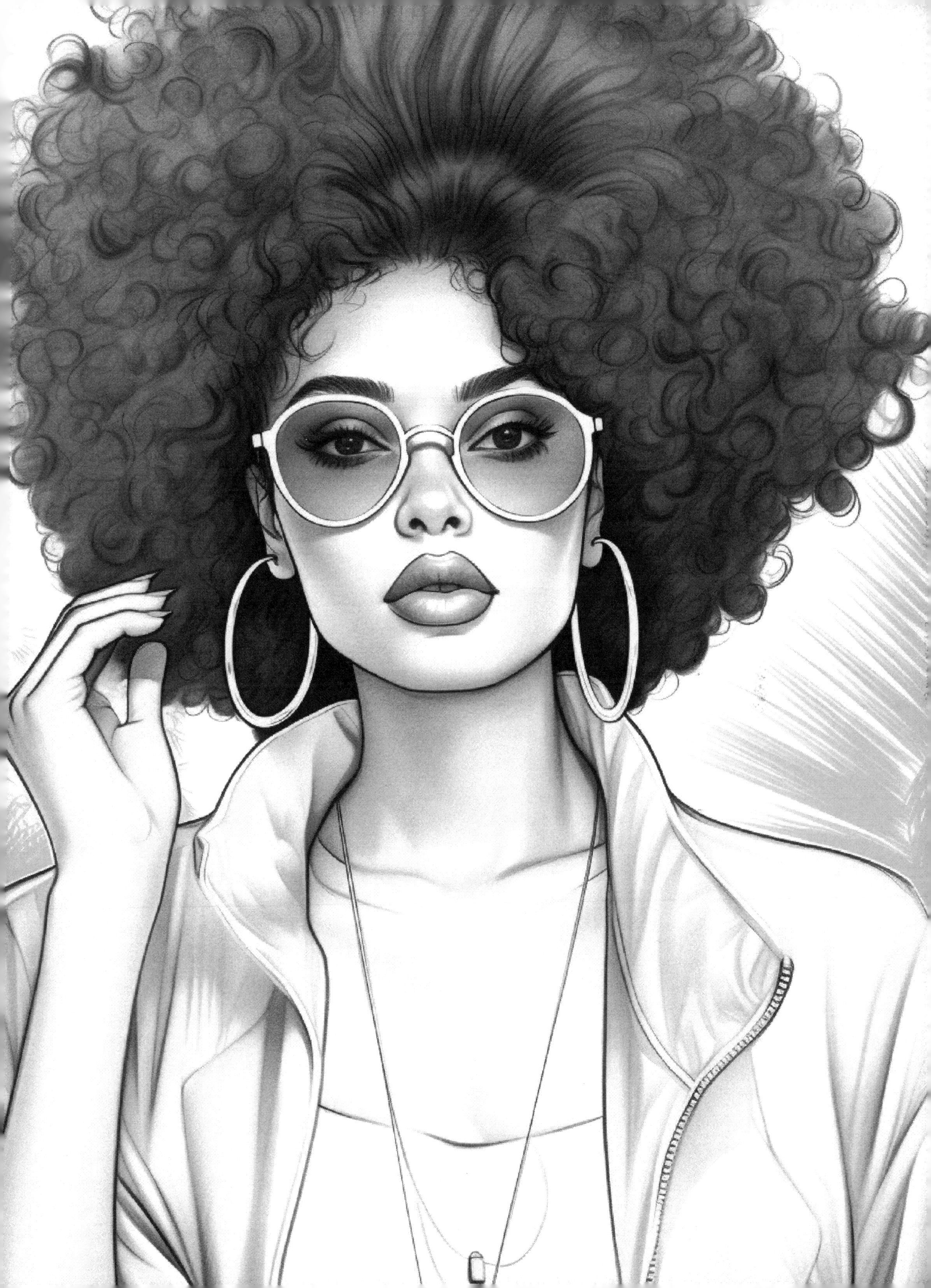

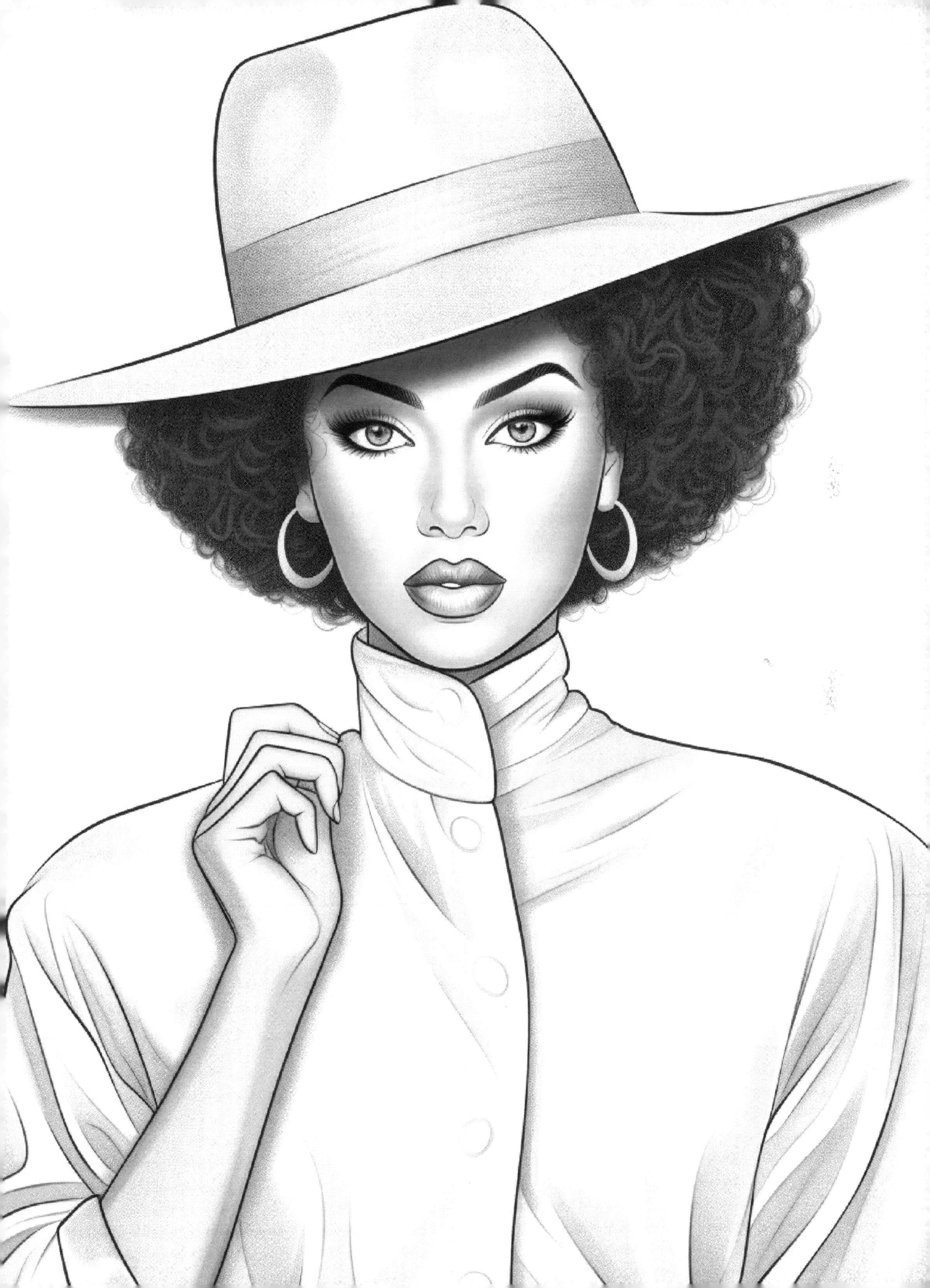

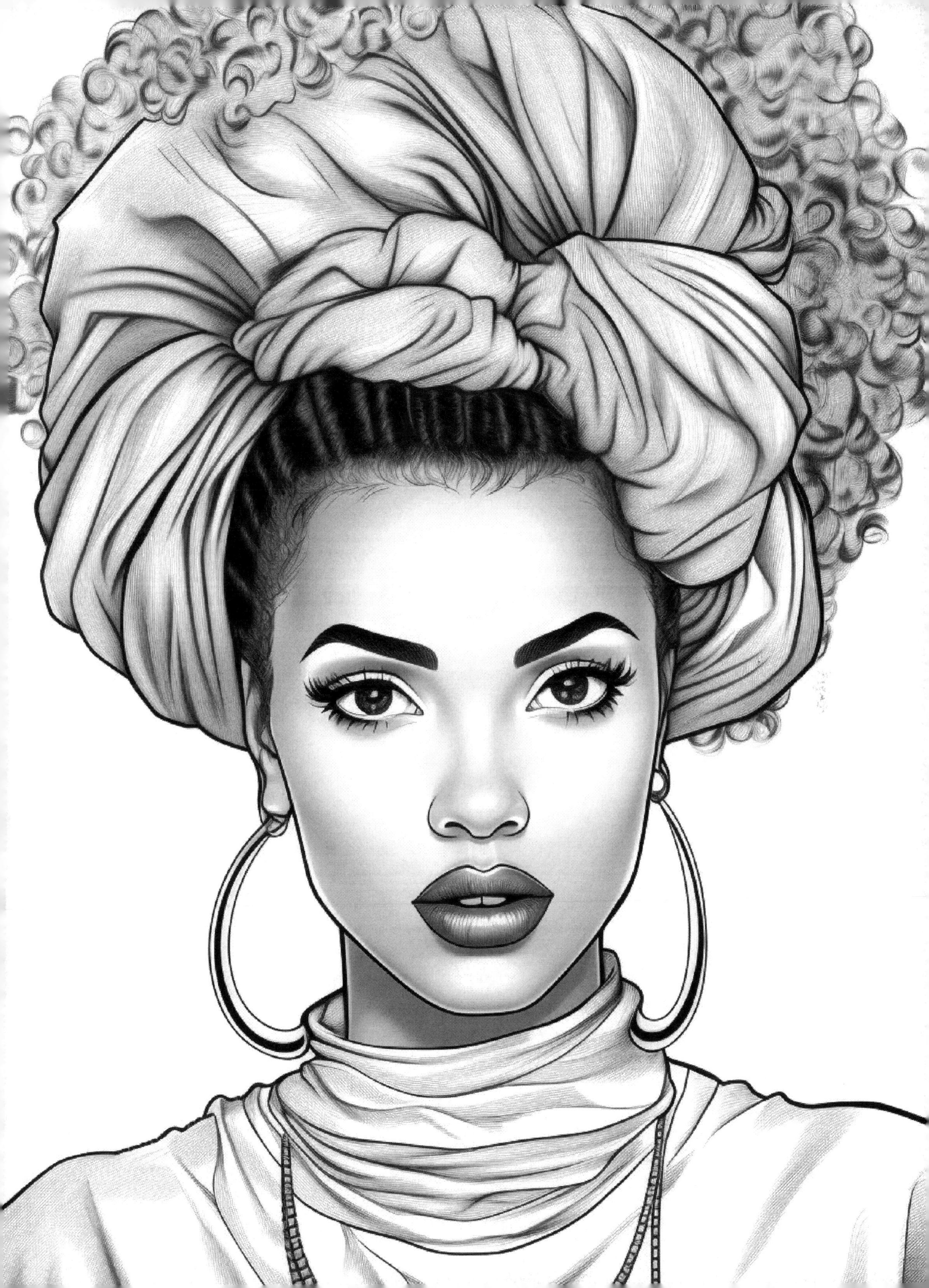

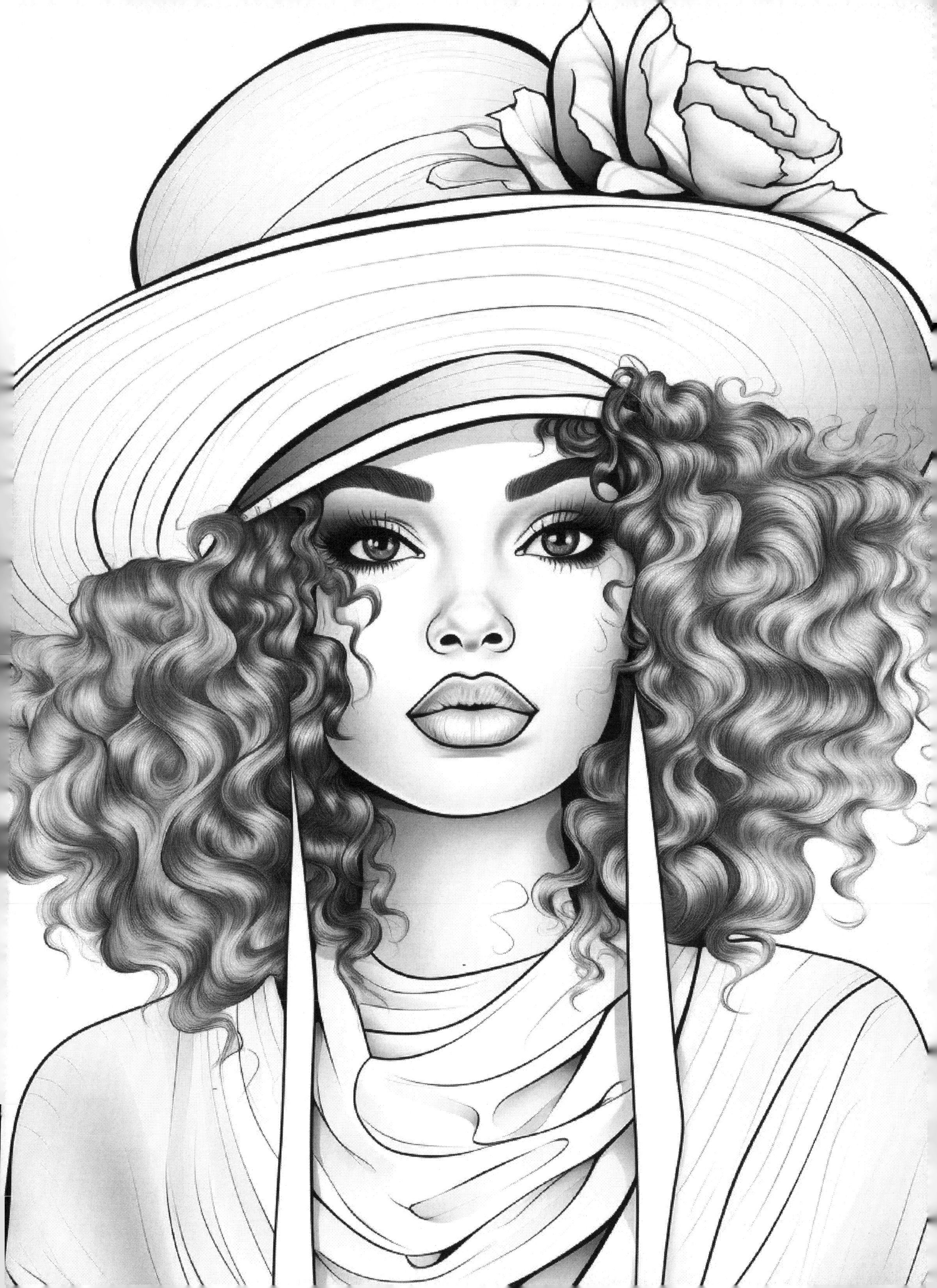

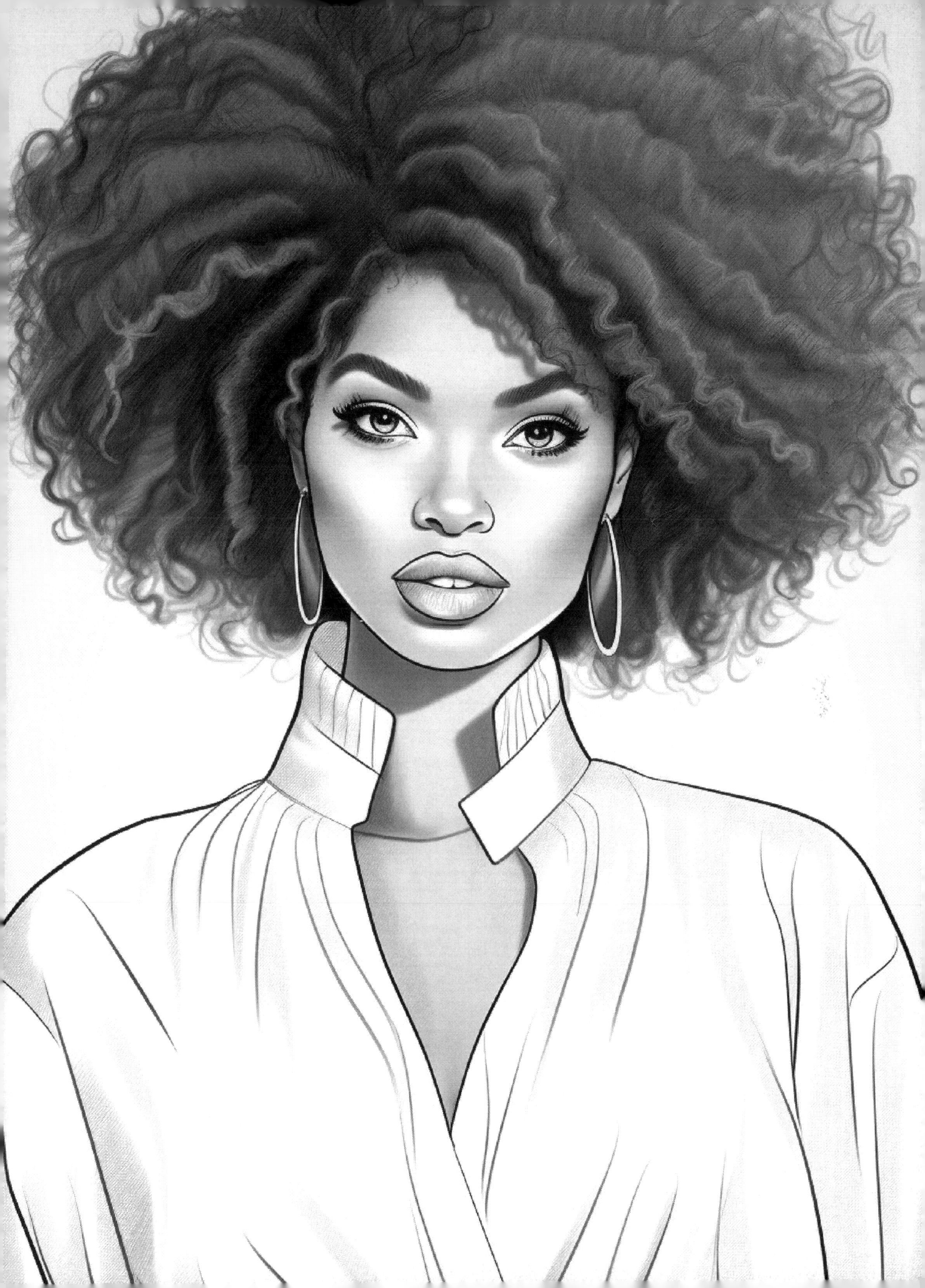

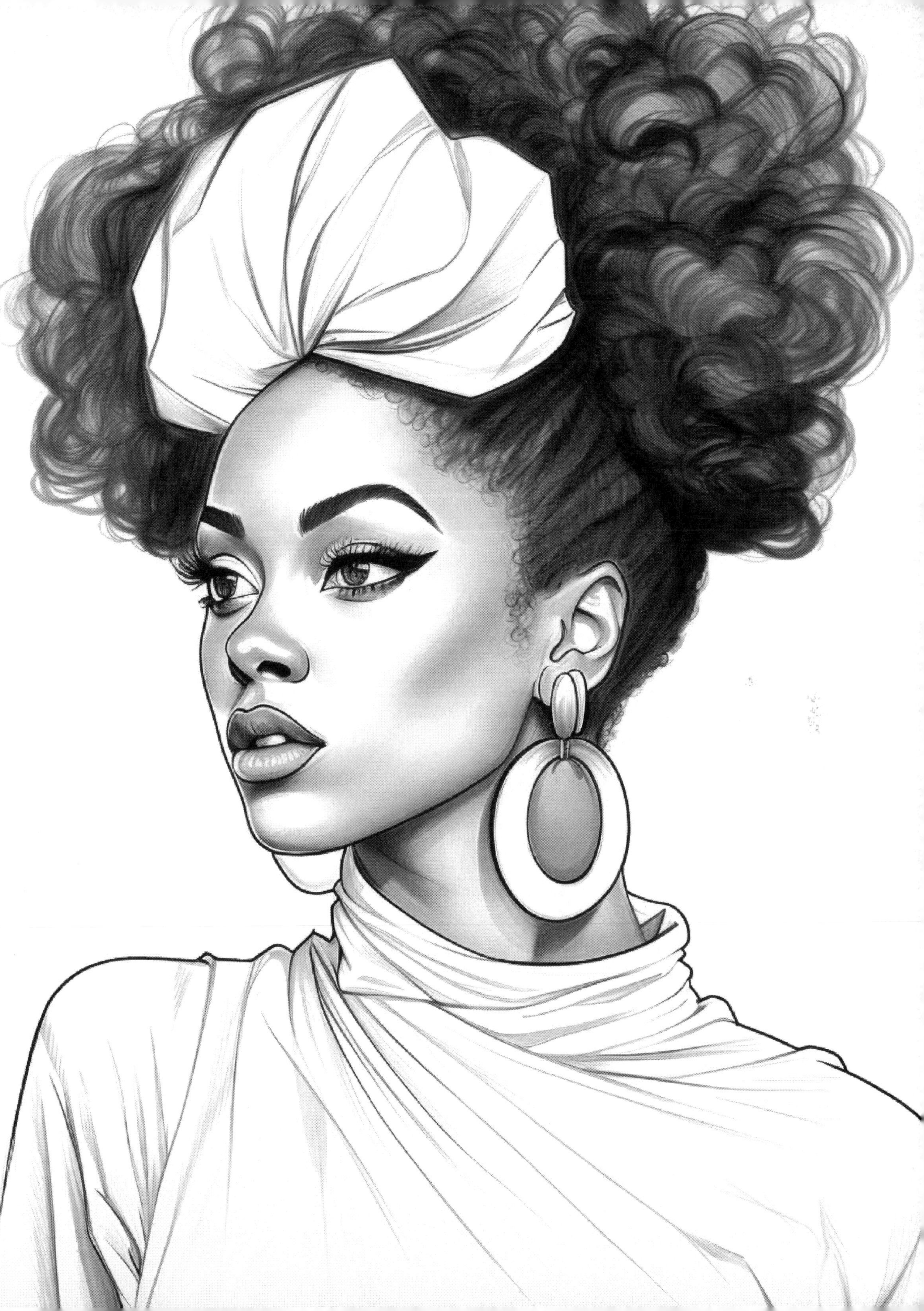

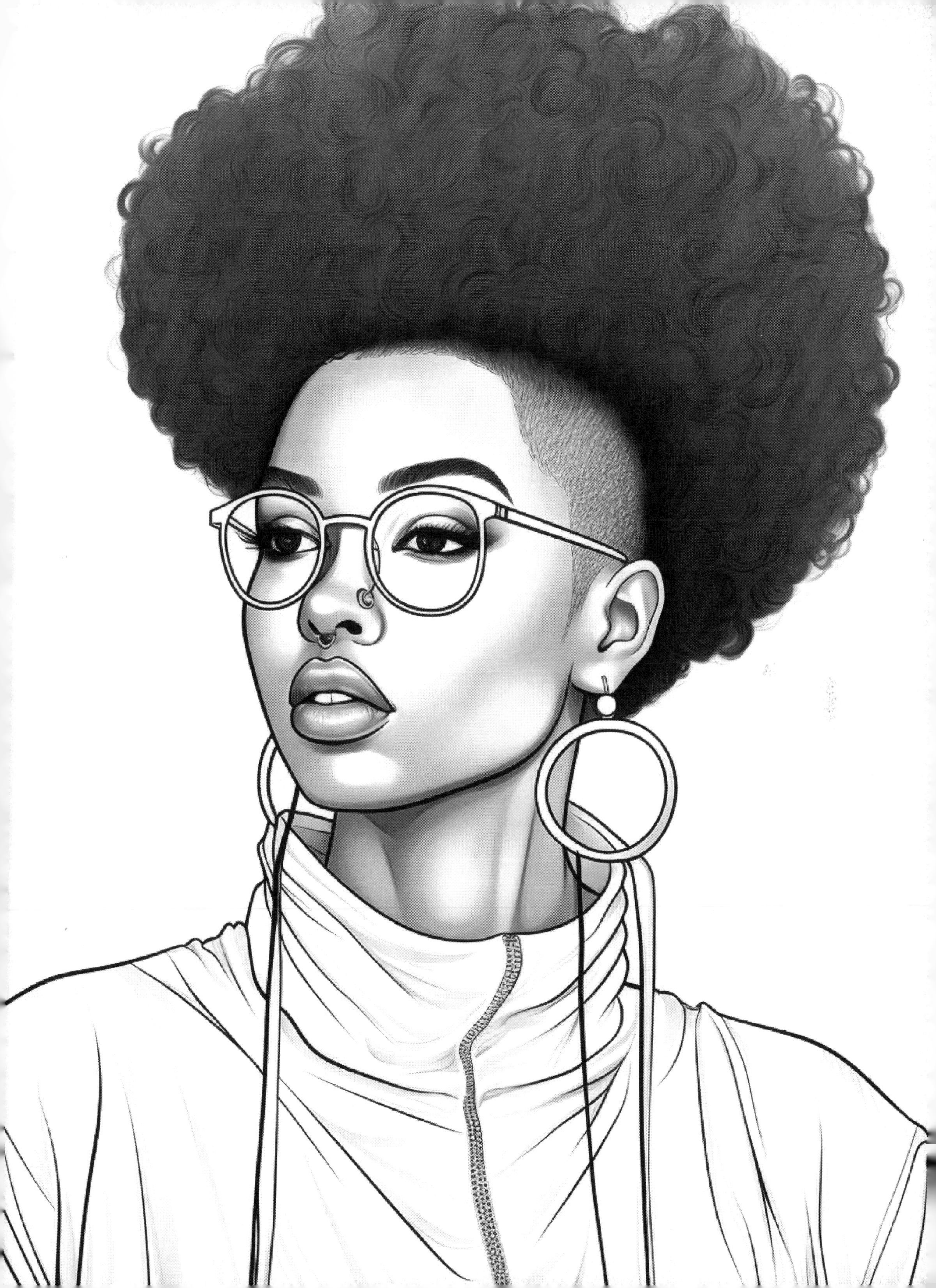

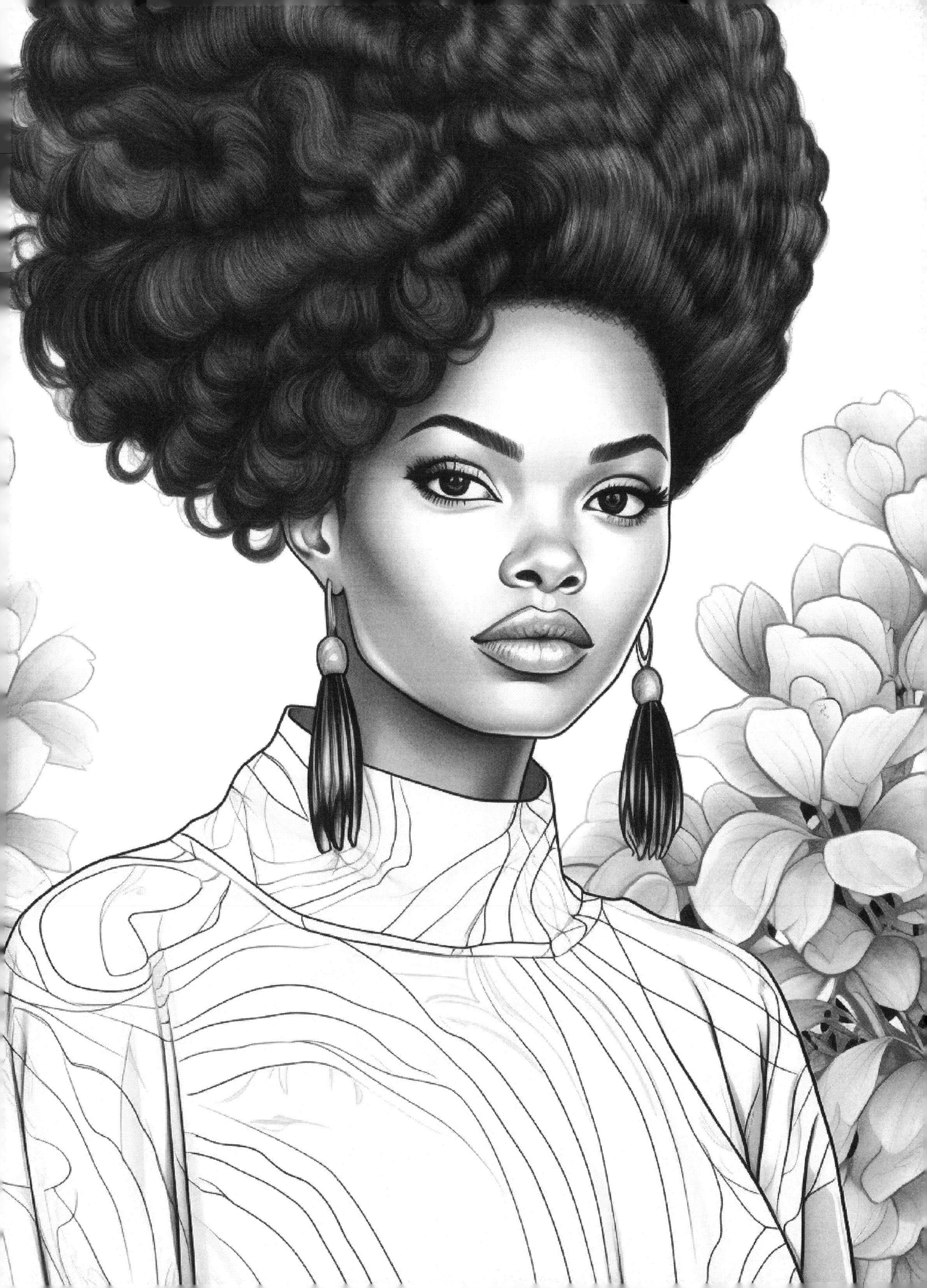

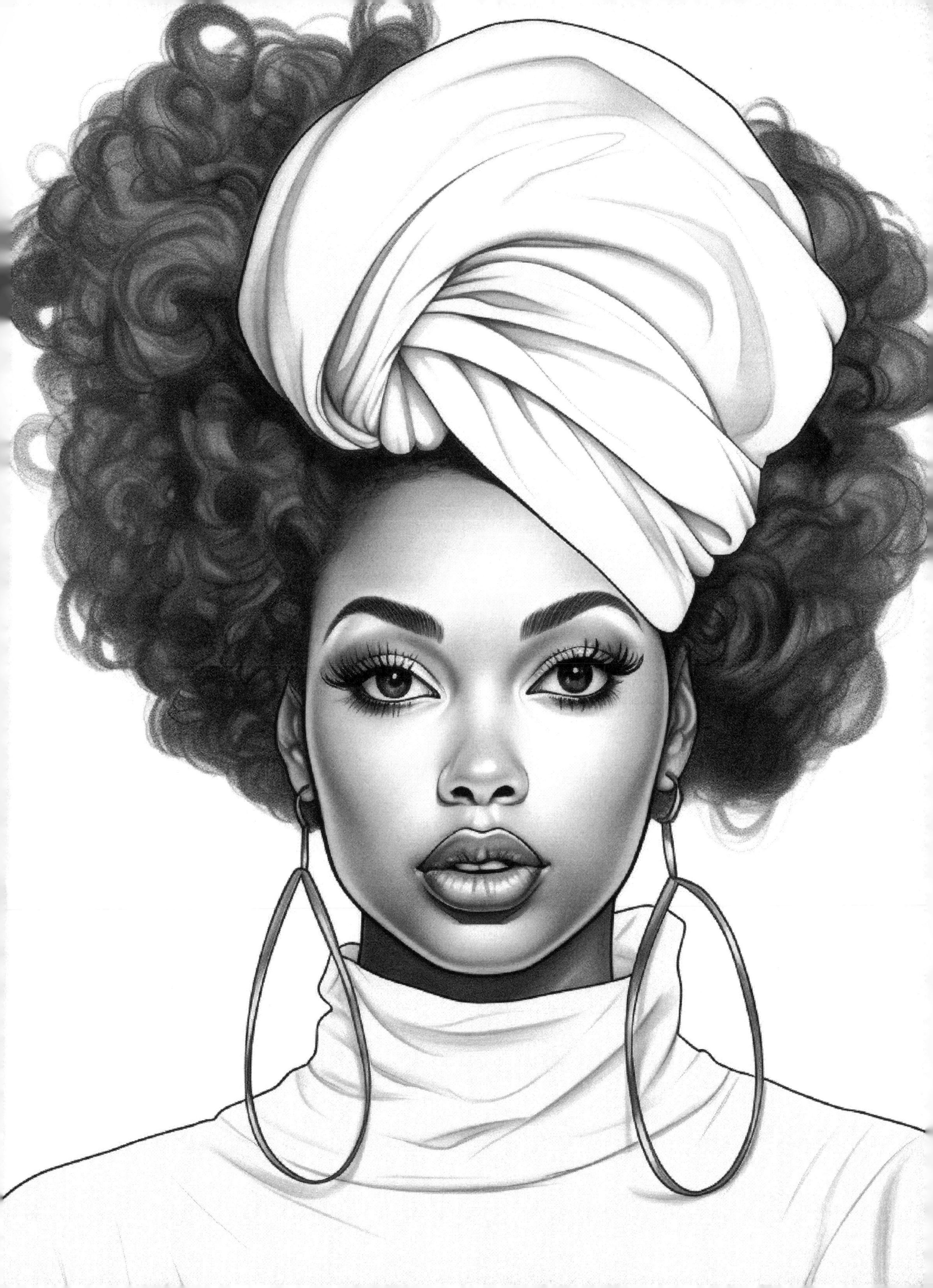

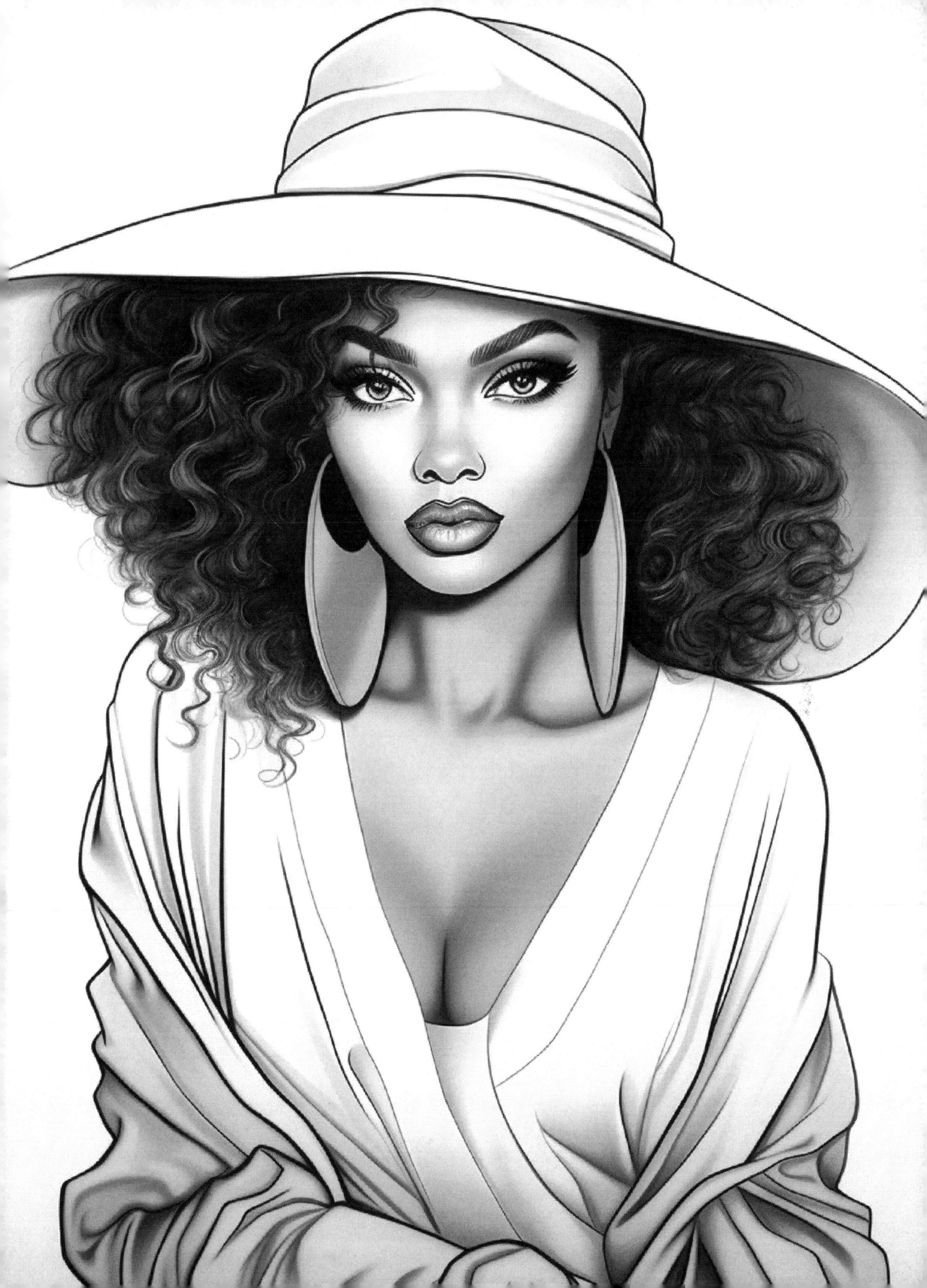

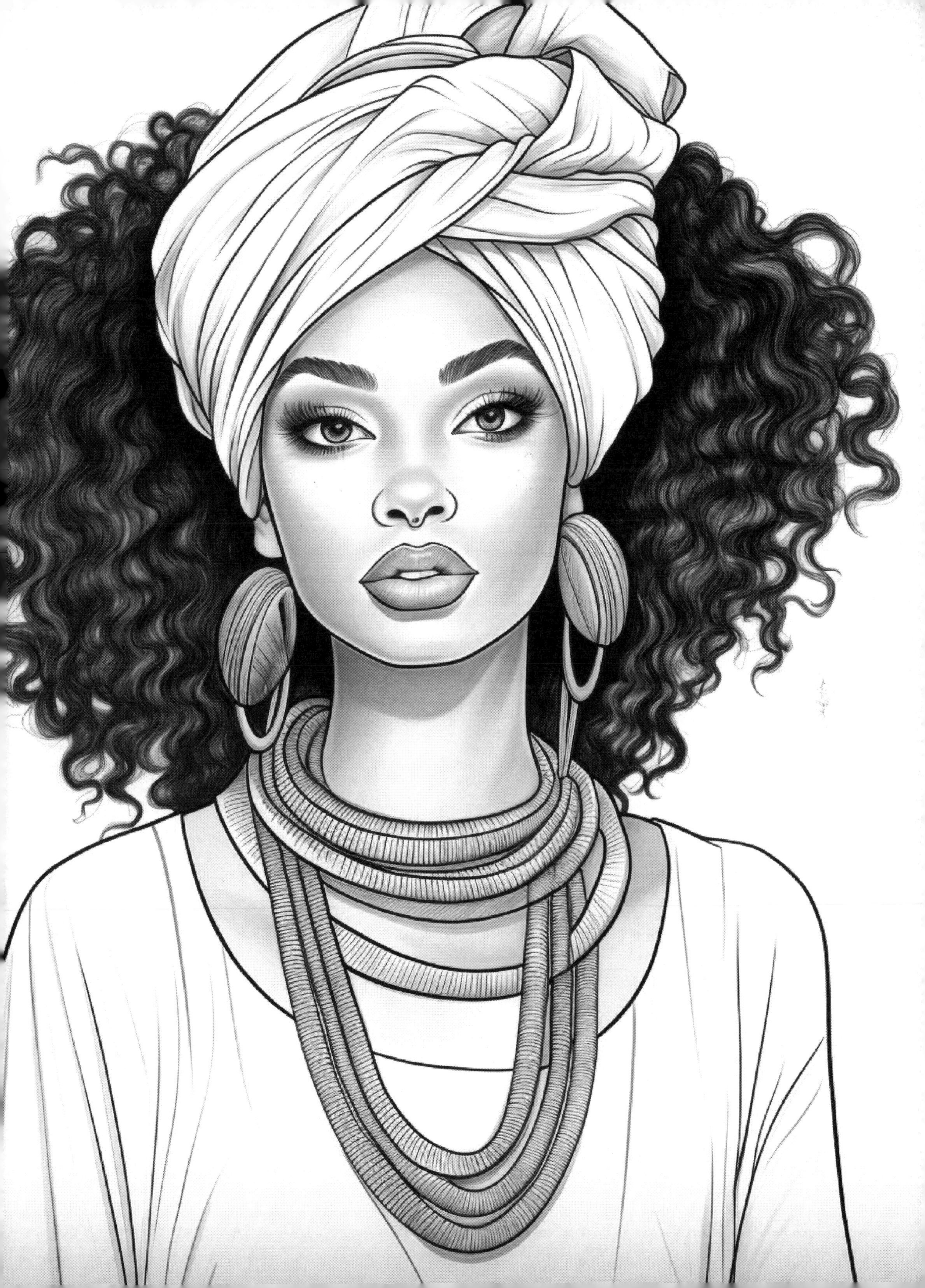

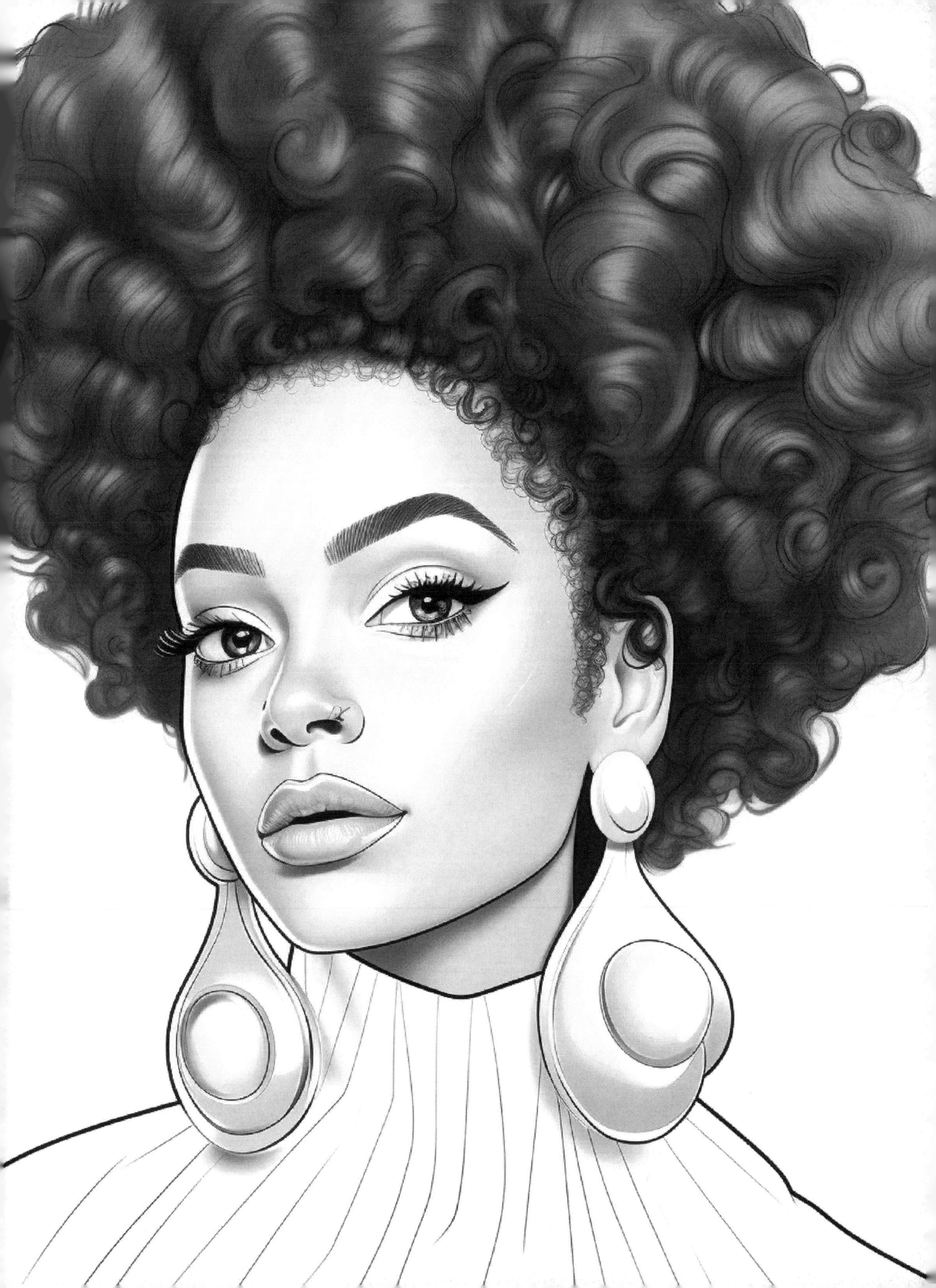

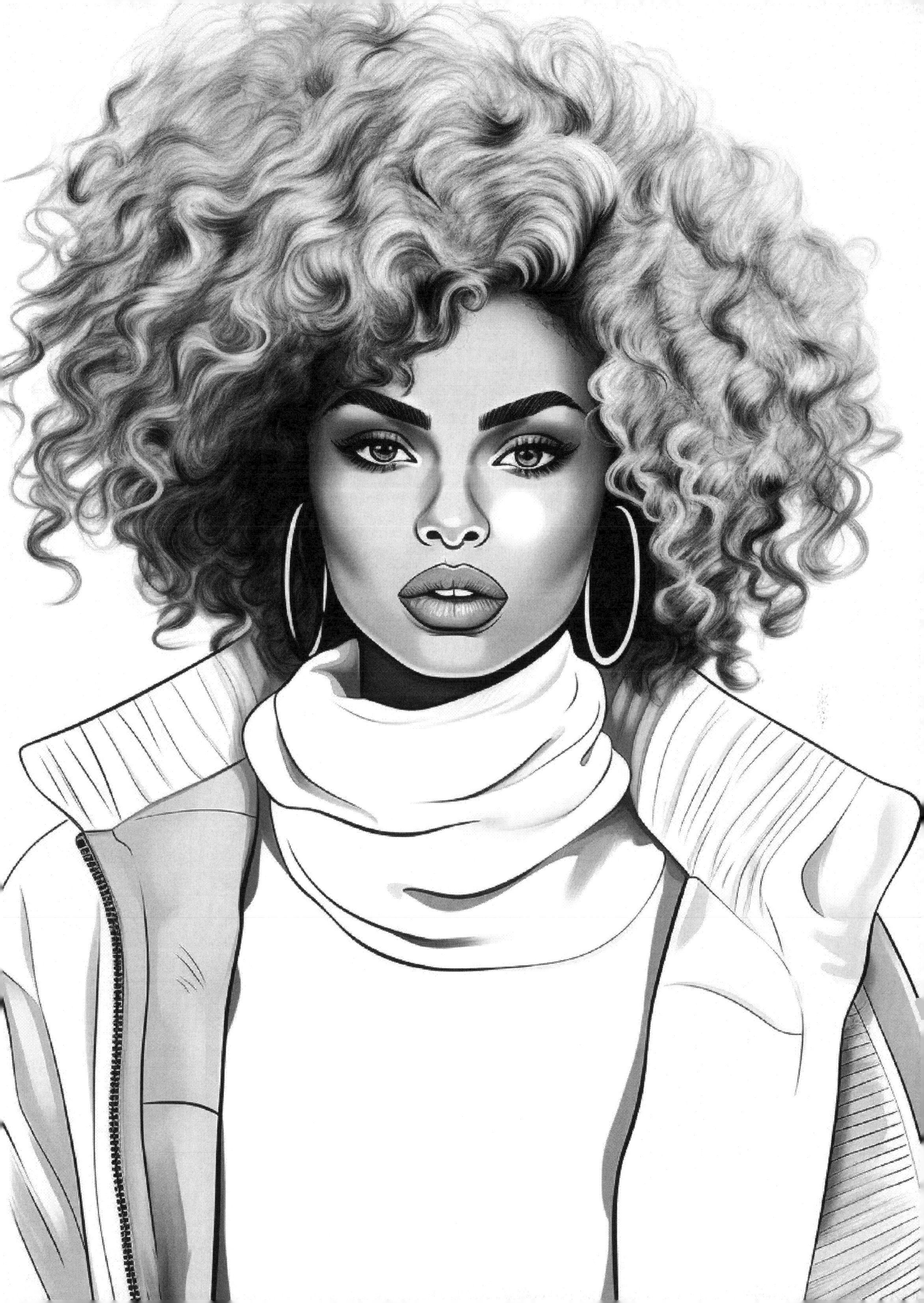

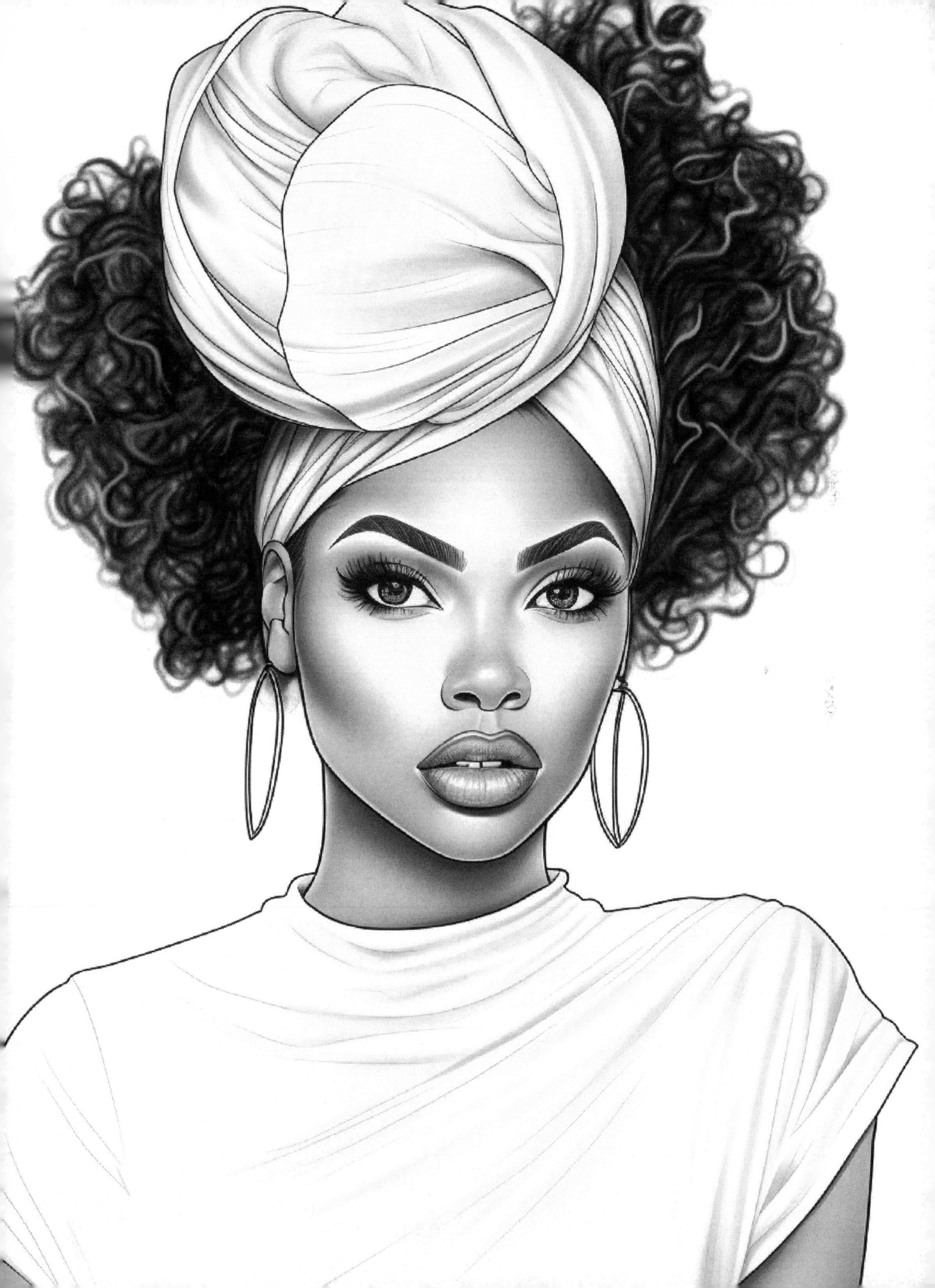

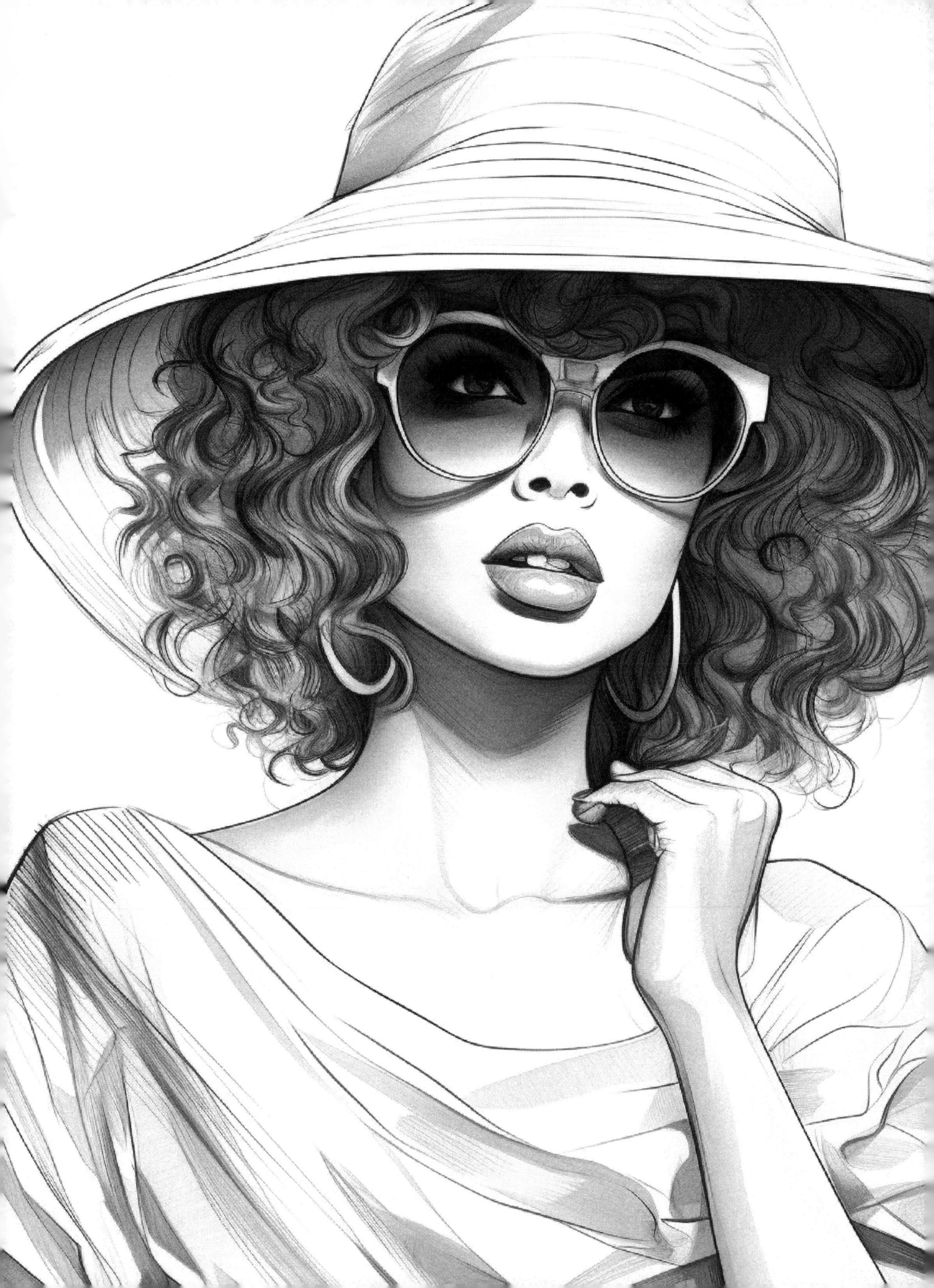

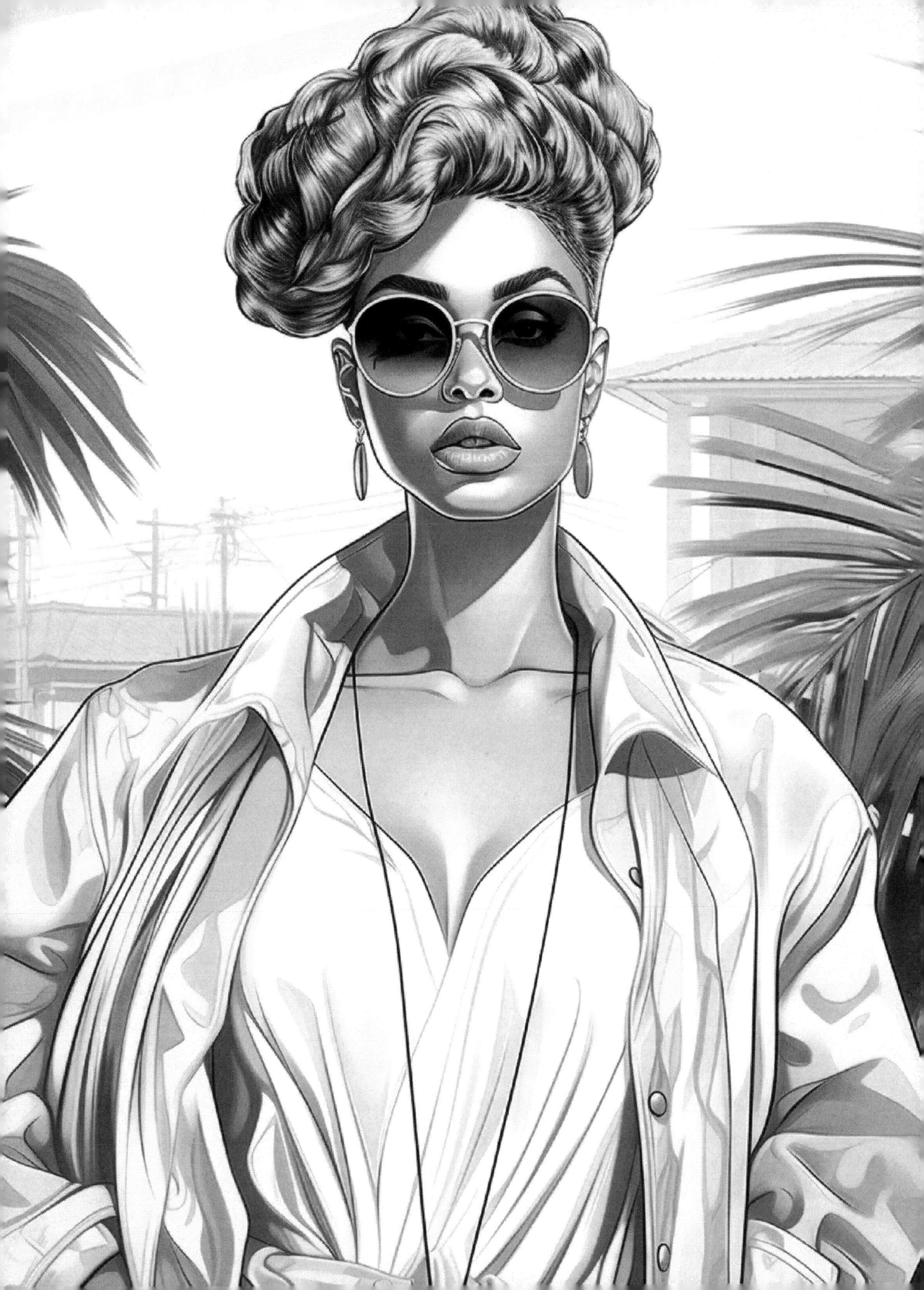

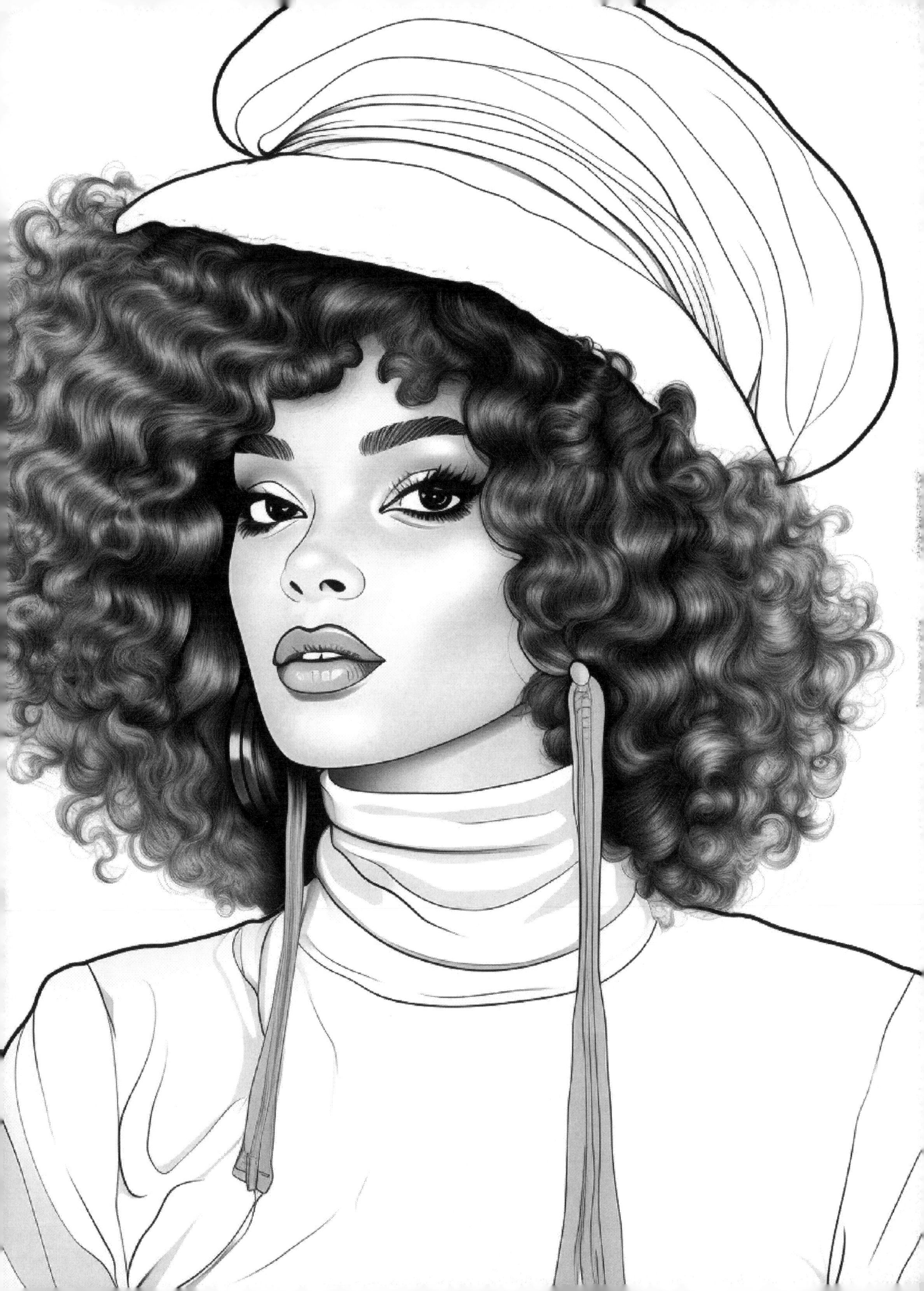

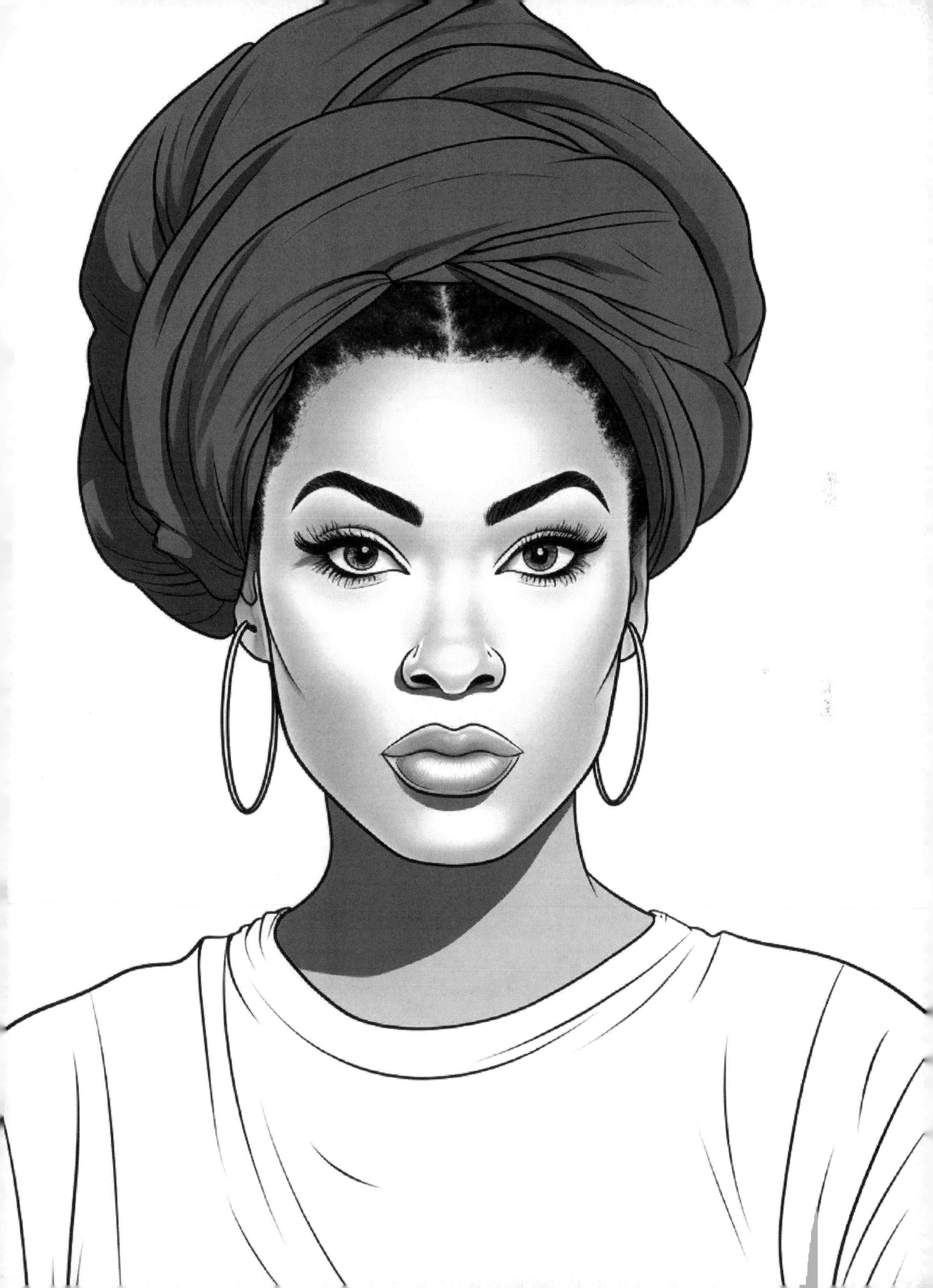

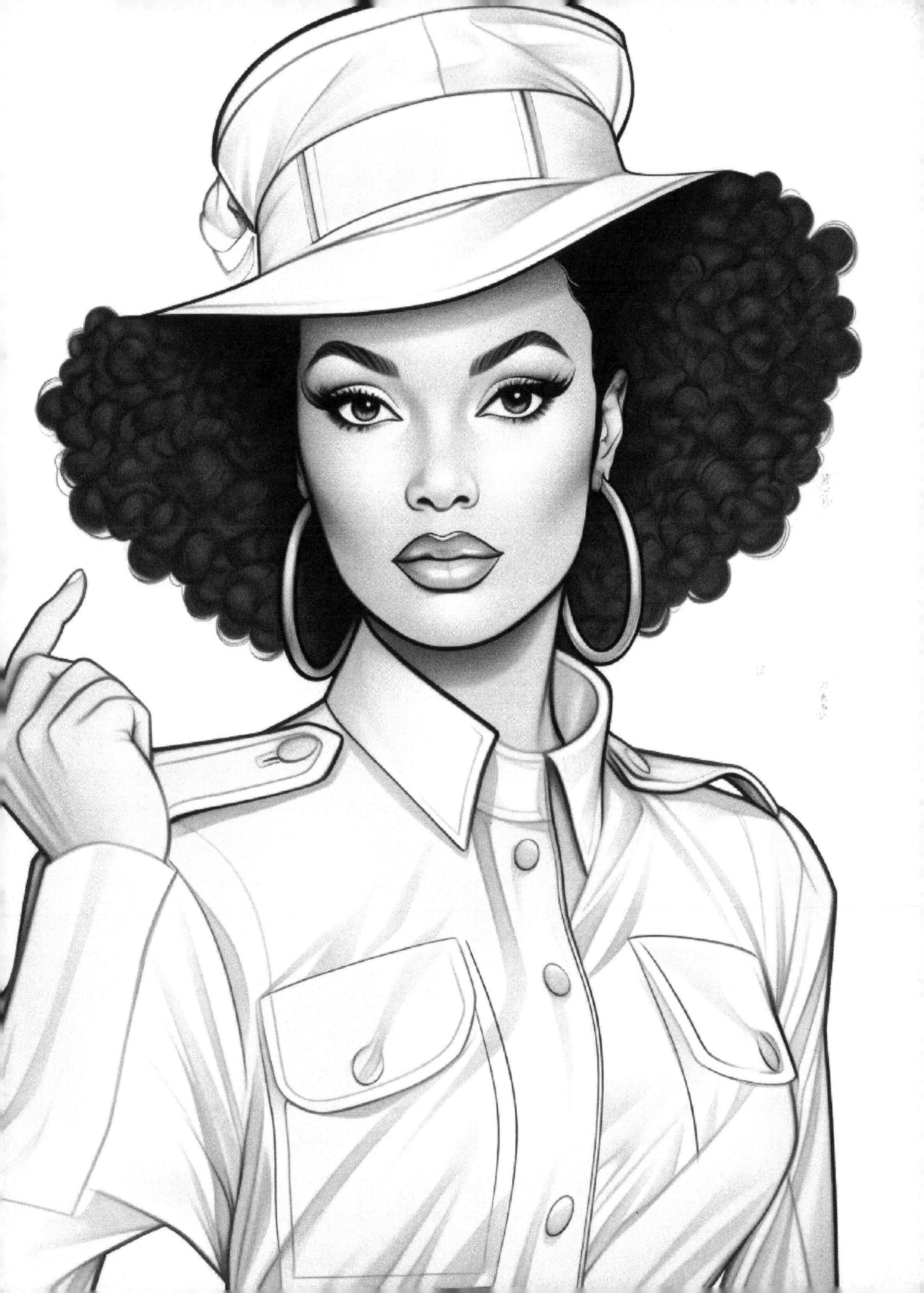

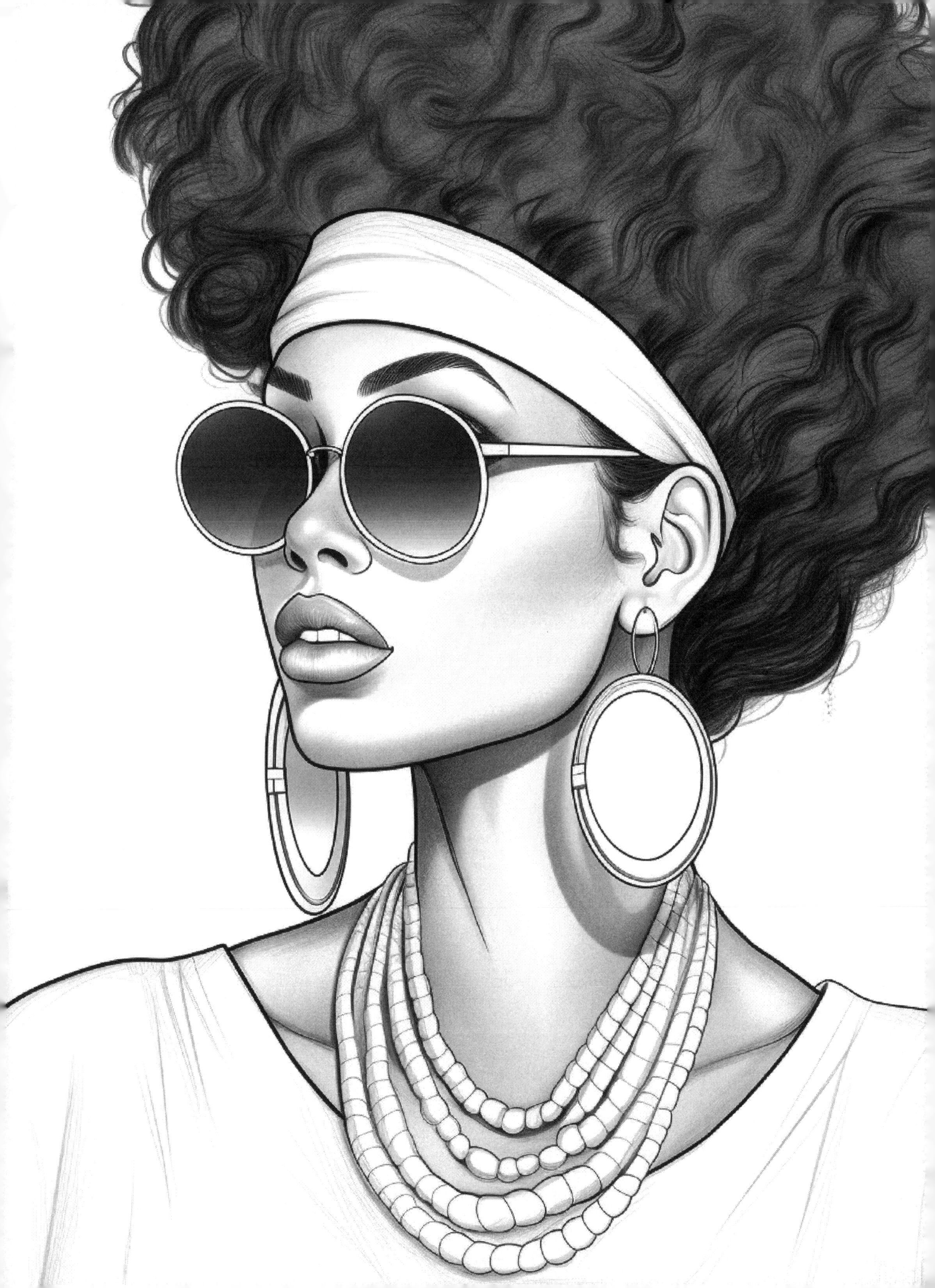

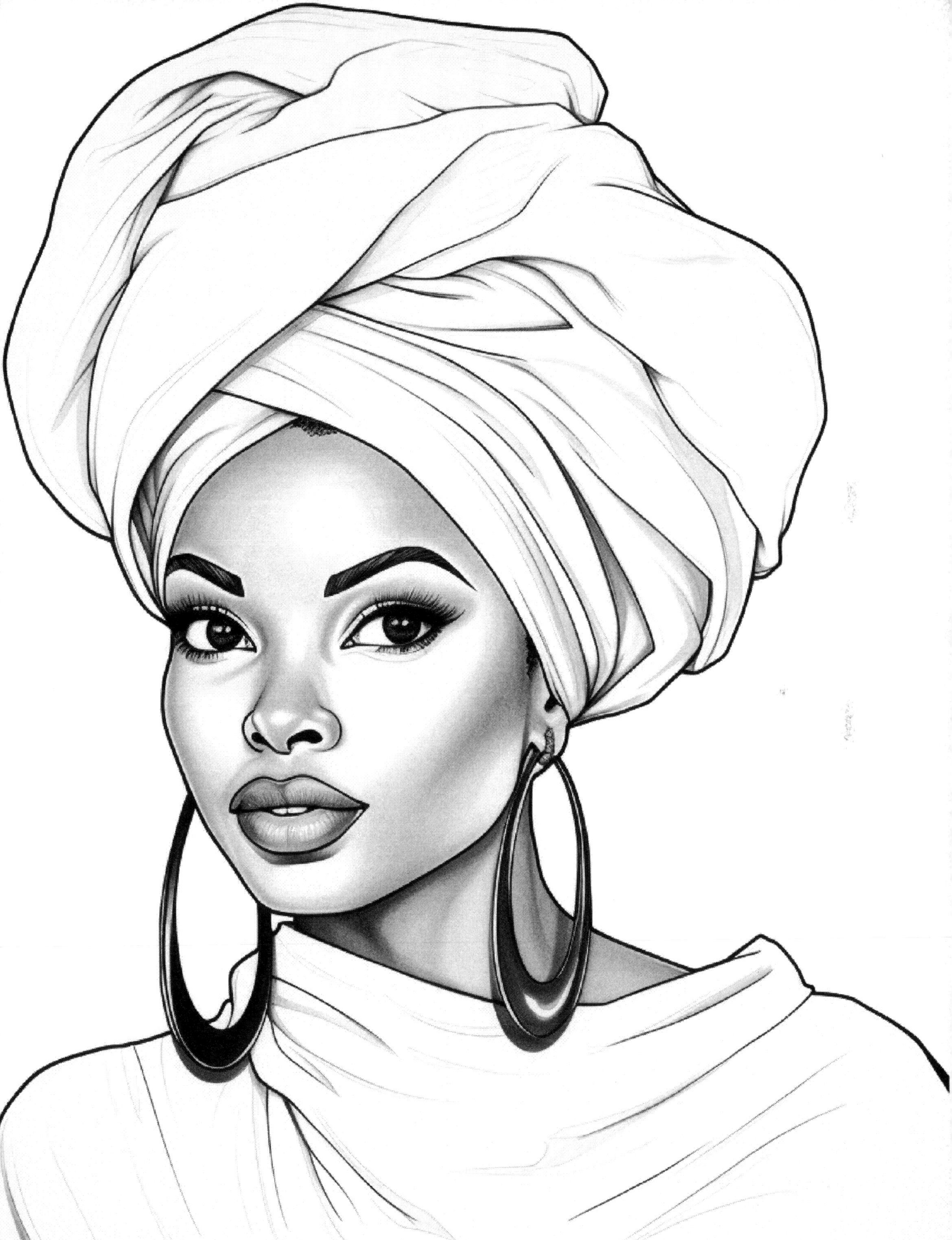

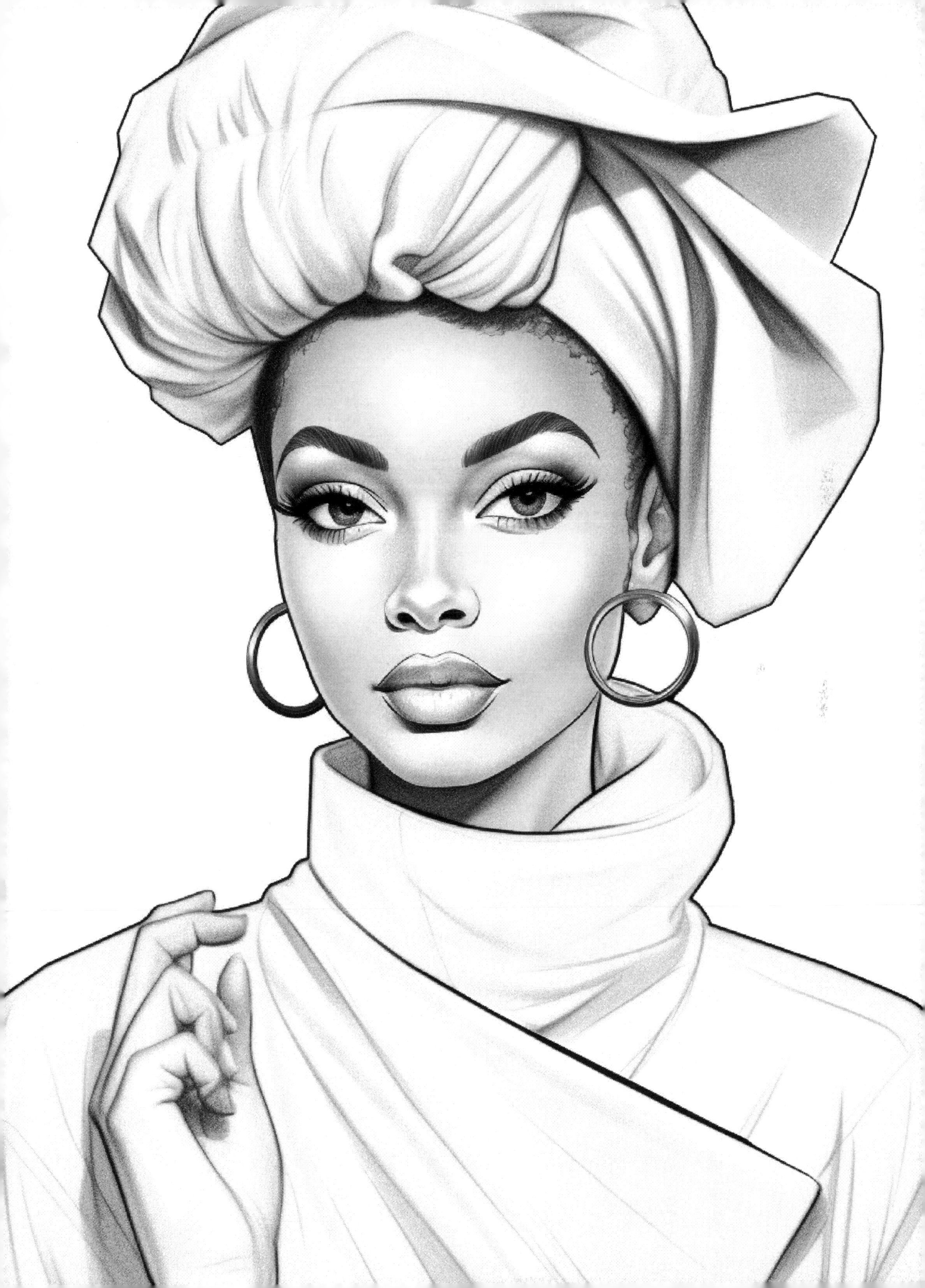

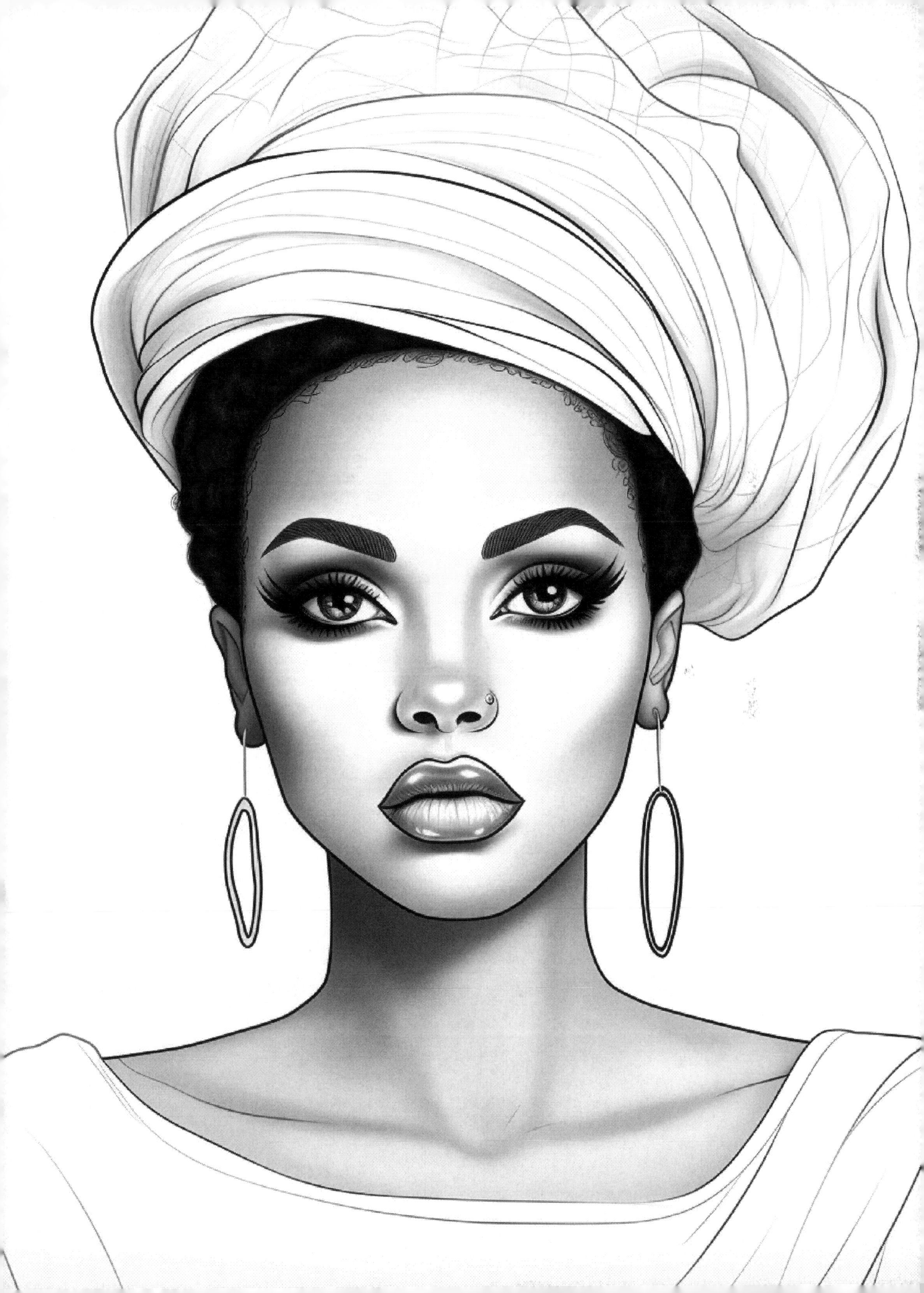

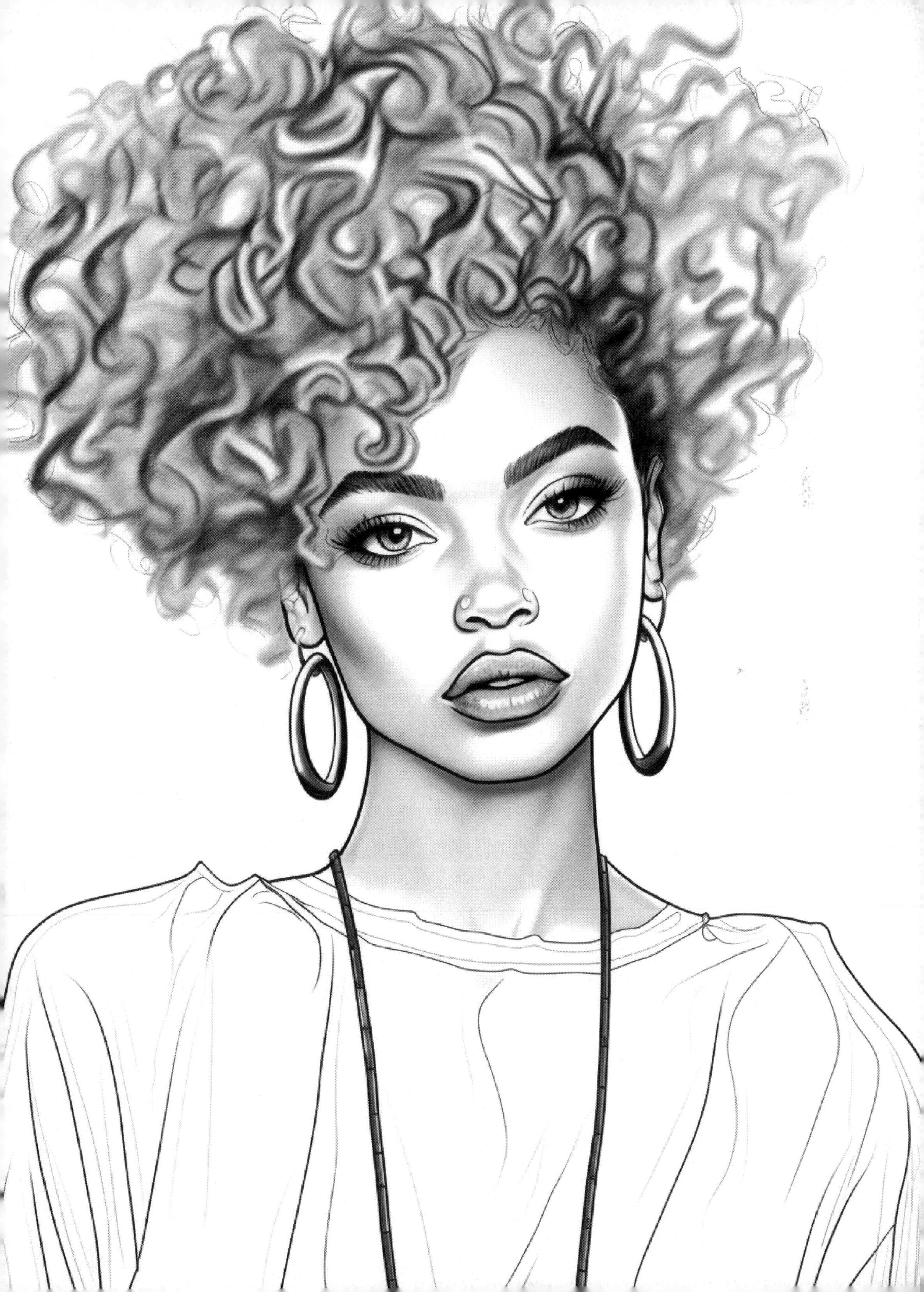

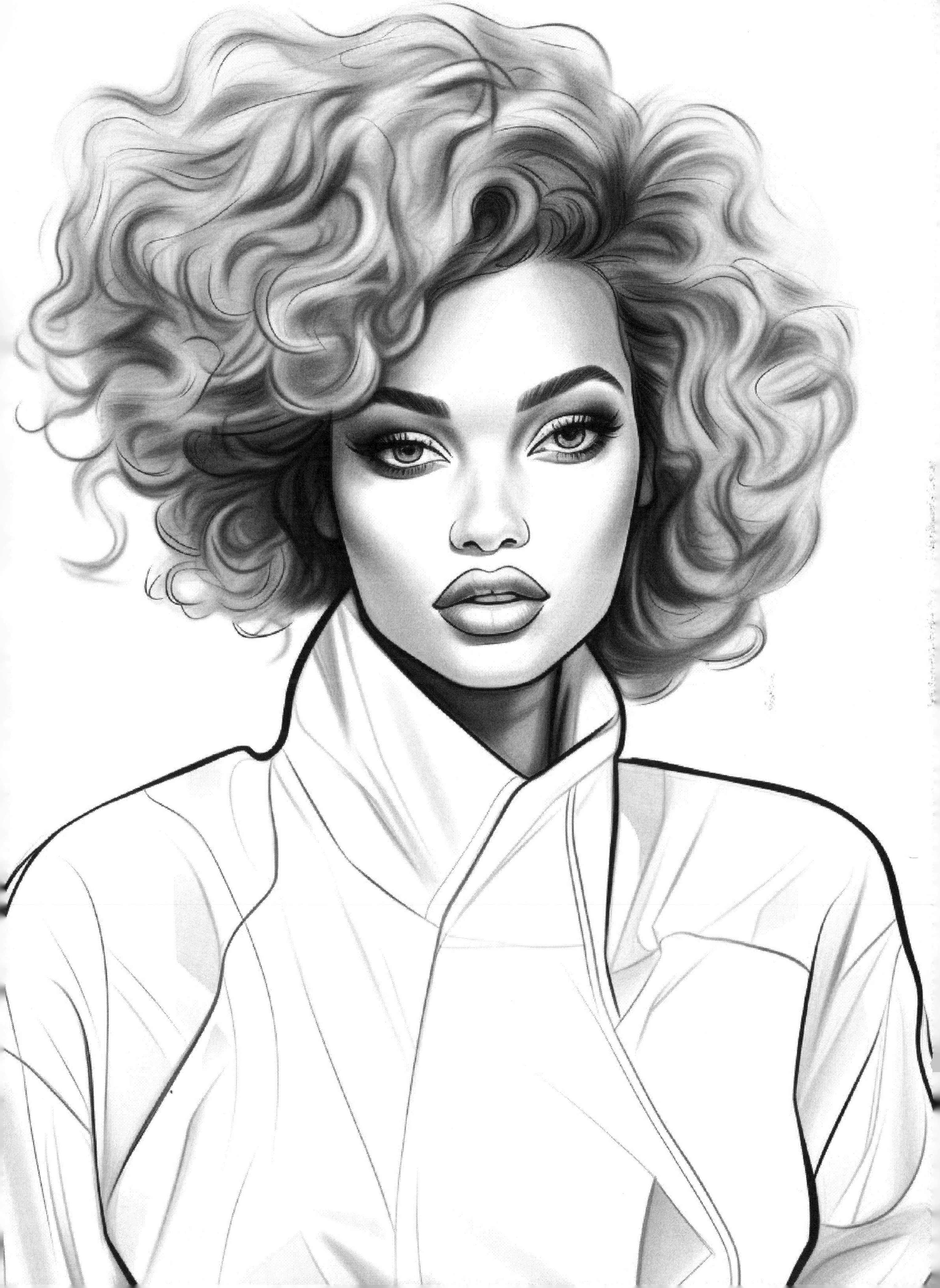

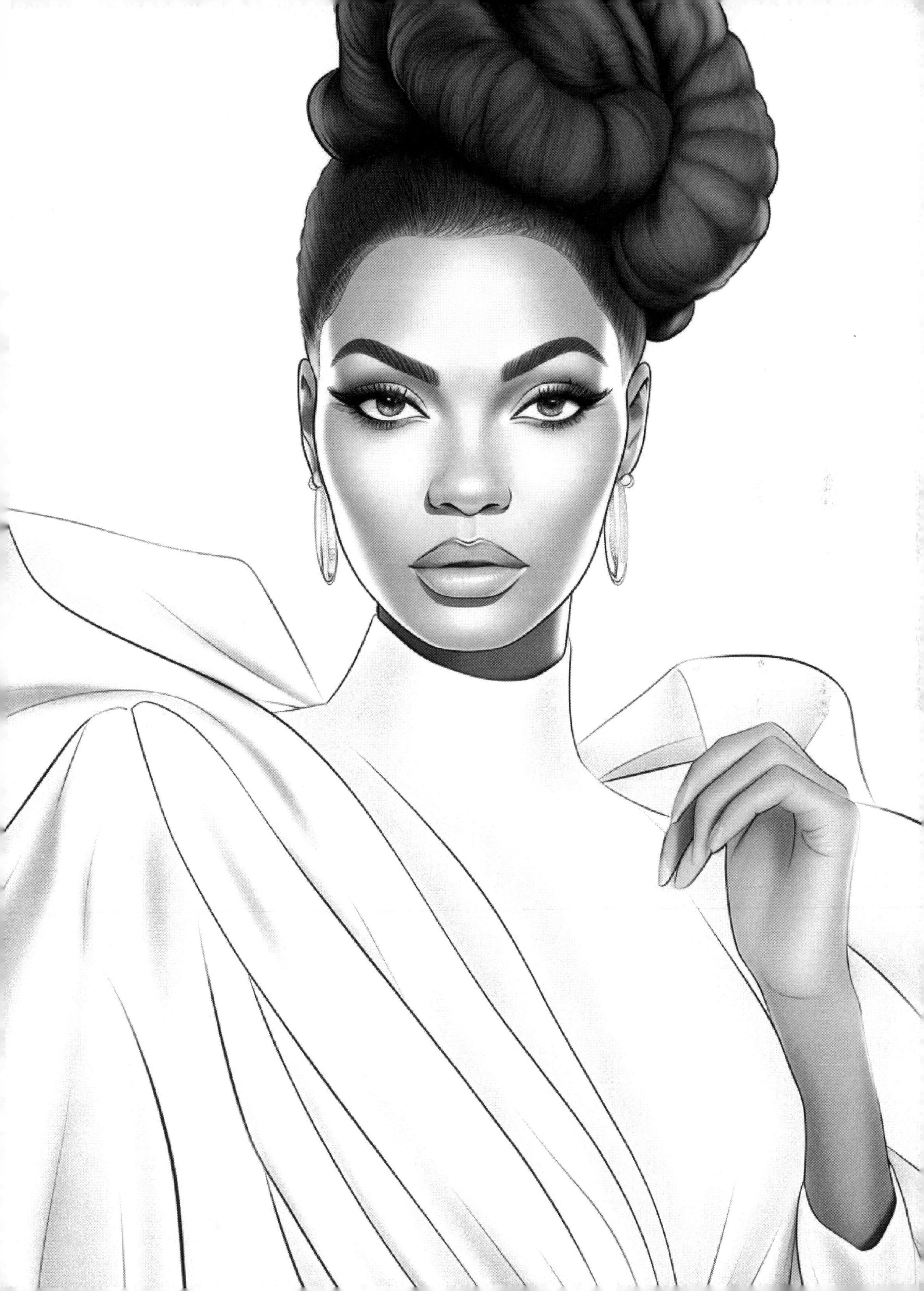

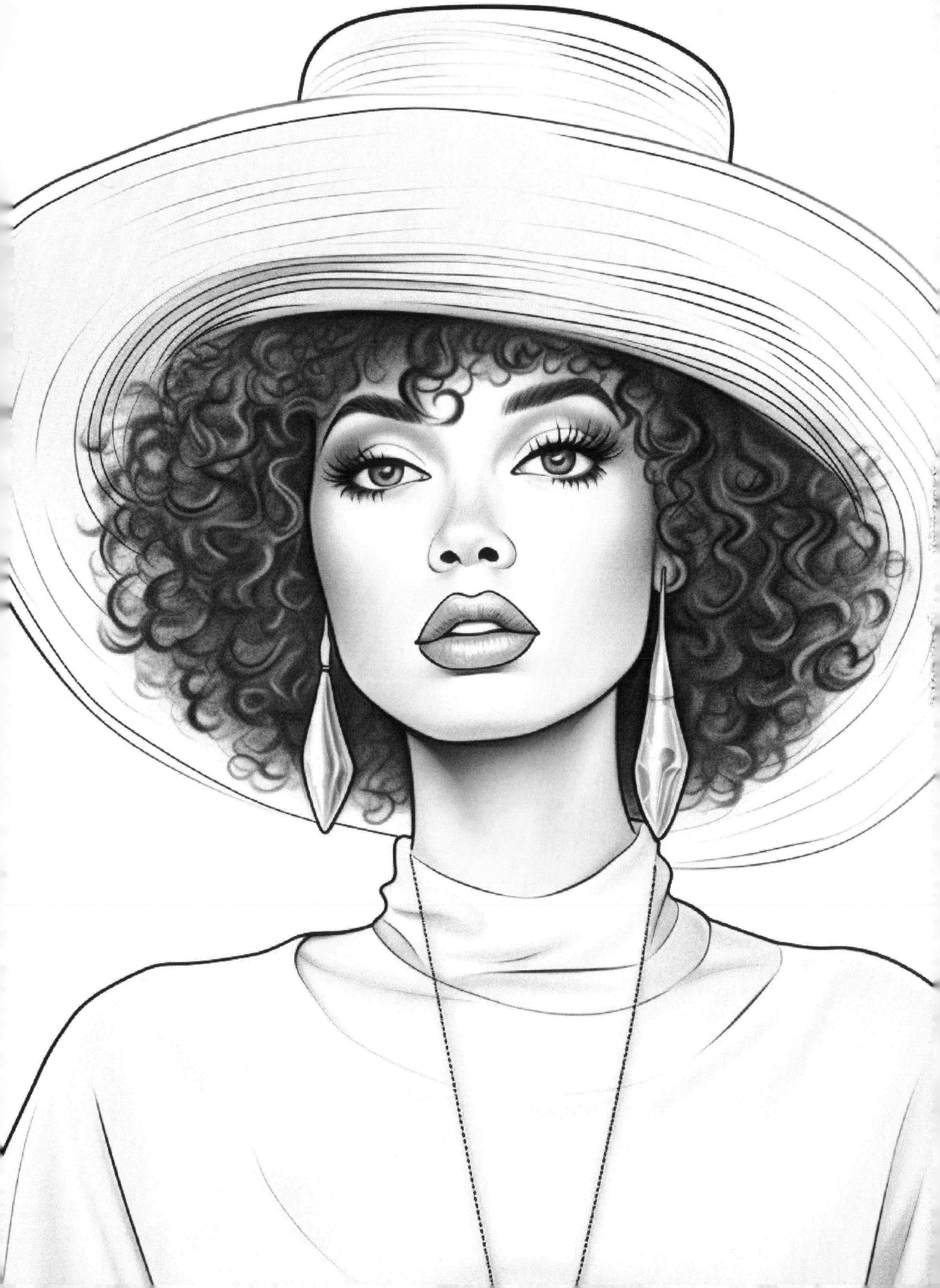

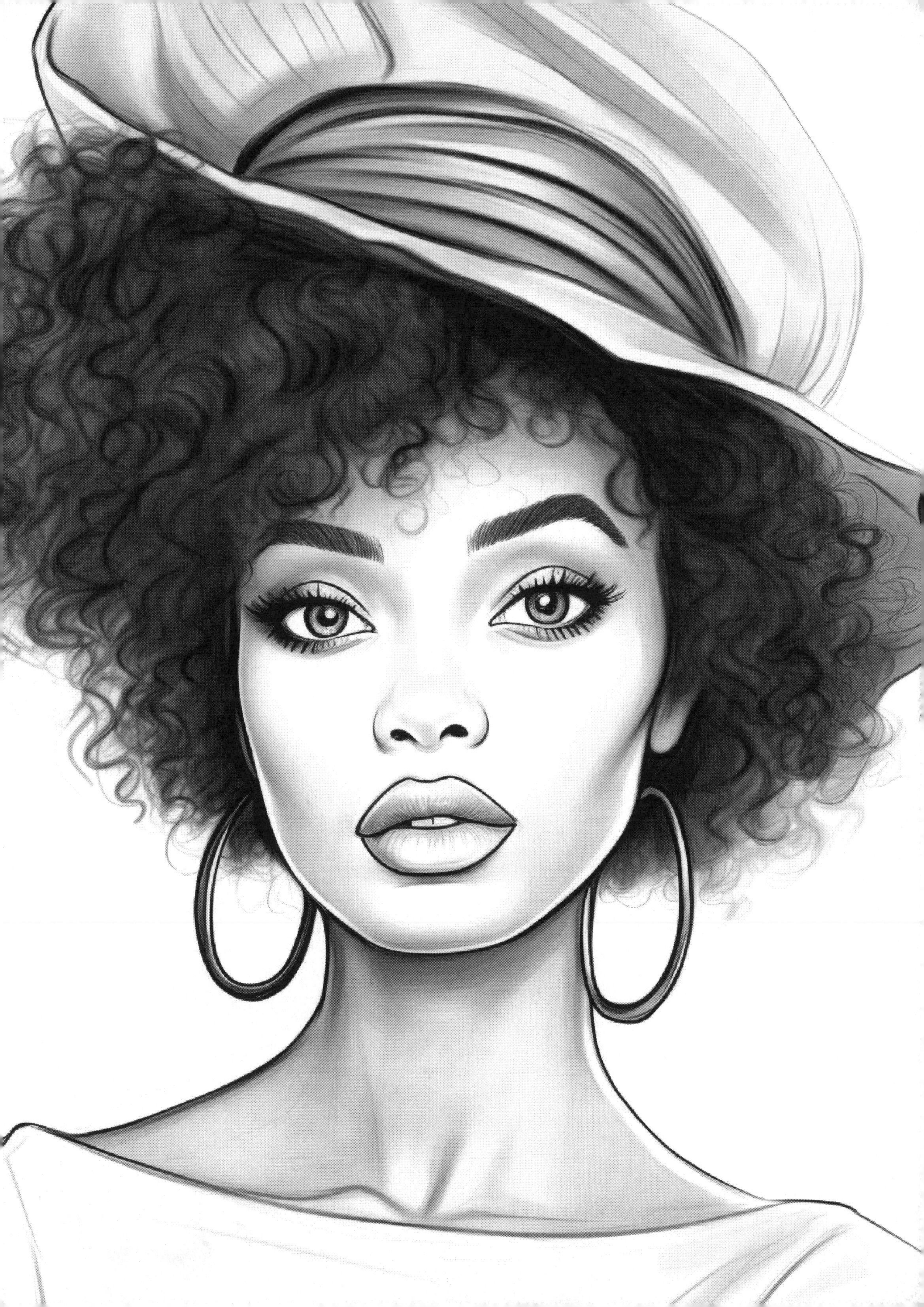